# The
# Management
# Skills
# Builder

# THE MANAGEMENT SKILLS BUILDER

## Self-Directed Learning Strategies for Career Development

**RALPH S. HAMBRICK**

PRAEGER

New York
Westport, Connecticut
London

Library of Congress Cataloging-in-Publication Data

Hambrick, Ralph S.
   The management skills builder : self-directed learning
strategies for career development / Ralph S. Hambrick.
      p.   cm.
   Includes bibliographical references and index.
   ISBN 0-275-94051-9 (alk. paper)
   1. Business communication.   2. Research—Methodology.
I. Title.
   HF5718.H283   1991
   658.4'5—dc20          91-7457

British Library Cataloguing in Publication Data is available.

Library of Congress Catalog Card Number: 91-7457
ISBN: 0-275-94051-9

First published in 1991

Praeger Publishers, One Madison Avenue, New York, NY 10010
An imprint of Greenwood Publishing Group, Inc.

Printed in the United States of America

The paper used in this book complies with the
Permanent Paper Standard issued by the National
Information Standards Organization (Z39.48-1984).

10  9  8  7  6  5  4  3  2  1

# Contents

# Preface

Talent, knowledge, and hard work do not guarantee success in a managerial or professional career, although they certainly contribute. Competent, knowledgeable, and hard-working people often have less impact and achieve less career success than they would seem to deserve. Sometimes the missing ingredient for success is a set of fundamental skills, skills that give talent, knowledge, and hard work leverage and visibility.

## THE SKILL ADVANTAGE

The manager and professional who can write efficiently and well; who is an effective and willing public speaker; who can interview effectively and uses that skill regularly; who can and does relate effectively with others, both individually and in group settings; who is personally able to use a computer; and who can tap into the burgeoning volume of information with some precision to solve problems and to update professional knowledge, has a greater probability of success than one who cannot or does not. The mastery of these skills may make the difference between mediocrity and excellence in professional and managerial performance and the recognition the performance receives. The lack of these skills may mean poor performance, quality performance poorly displayed, or opportunities for making an impact by-passed. Since managerial and professional education often pay little attention to these skills that enable an individual to shine in the workplace, those people who develop them on their own have a strong advantage over those who do not.

I hope readers will use this book with two purposes in mind. The first is mastery of the six specific skills. Each one has a clear potential for enhancing career success *and* career satisfaction. A manager or professional who is competent and accomplished at writing, speaking, interviewing, relating, computing, and searching has important foundations for excellent performance and for excellent performance that will be noticed. Additionally, these skills add to satisfaction not just because they enhance career success, but because they enable the accomplishment of specific tasks with style and quality. These skills can give the same sense of satisfaction that comes from a baseball well hit, a pot well thrown, a piano well played, a picture well painted, a ski run well executed. So each skill has the potential for rewards that are both extrinsic (position, promotion, pay) and intrinsic (enjoyment, pride, satisfaction).

The second purpose for reading the book is learning how to learn any new skill. The manager or professional who is adept at developing new skills is more likely to be successful than one who is not. The most successful and satisfying career is likely to be characterized by the development of new skills and the honing of existing ones. Some of these skills may be career related, some not. Some may be highly job specific and others more generic, like the ones addressed in this book.

Two key ideas permeate the approach to skill development presented here. First is the idea of designing your own skill-development plan. Some self reflection and planning can produce an approach particularly tailored to your own needs and preferences. A self-designed and tailored approach has a better chance of succeeding than one invented elsewhere. Second, the theme is developed throughout the book that many skills, especially the fundamental ones, can be developed during activities that we already do. Most of us let untold opportunities for important skill development slip by. A simple shift in perspective and a conscious decision to learn can change a daily occurrence into a skill-learning opportunity.

## A NOTE ABOUT AUDIENCE

This book is intended primarily for practicing managers and professionals. It offers guidance in the development of skills that make a difference whether you are working in a large organization or as an individual entrepreneur, whether you are just beginning or are well along in your career. Skill development, including these generic skills, is not something that is accomplished once and for all.

While designed for practicing managers and professionals the book should also be useful for students, especially those planning a career in management or one of the professions. It can be used as an individual self-help tool or as a supplementary text in a variety of courses. These are skills students can practice and use while still in school as well as after their formal education.

The phrase "managers and professionals" is used at times in the book. In some ways it is redundant to use both terms since professionals are also managers, at least to some degree, and managers are professionals. The use of both is warranted, however, since most people identify more closely with one label or the other.

## A PERSONAL NOTE

These generic skills have become a matter of great interest to me for several reasons. The first and perhaps most important is my own sense of need to become more proficient in their use. In my career and personal life, I have had a growing desire to be better at doing the things implied in this list of generic skills. Being better sometimes means producing a better "product," as in a public speech; sometimes it means doing things more quickly, as in getting a memorandum written in a timely fashion; and sometimes it means being able to converse intelligently with persons more skilled and knowledgeable than I am, for instance, in the field of computers.

The recognition by the professionals and administrators with whom I work of similar skill-development needs for themselves and those with whom they work is a second reason these generic skills have risen high on my attention list. Midcareer professionals with whom I have worked both on and off campus have stated concerns about the lack of these skills, sometimes about their personal lack and sometimes about the lack of these skills in others with whom they work and associate. One person might express a feeling of inadequacy in conducting some upcoming interviews; another might complain about the poor writing skill of subordinates in her office. One person might indicate that she does not have a clue about how to find the latest information about some topic at work; another complains about the poor job his department head did in briefing the legislative budget committee. The lack-of-skills complaint extends to the prominent as well. A comment made by a member of the audience after a presentation by a Nobel Laureate was: "I sure wish he had taken a course in public speaking." So those of us who can profit from skill development are in good company. The evidence is widespread that these (and other) skills are needed, but that many people, often quite knowledgeable in their own professional specialties, lack proficiency in their use.

The relative lack of knowledge or ideas about how to improve these skills also added to my interest in writing about them. I felt a need to improve my information-search skills, among others, but had no notion of how to go about it. That seems to be the case with others. Part of that inertia is simply lack of awareness of available resources and the steps that can be taken to improve skills. Both formal and informal opportunities for learning are sometimes readily available but often go unnoticed and unused. Books, workshops, seminars, free consultation, tutorials, seminars, cassette tapes, and more may be available but not noticed or at least not used by those who could profit.

Equally to the point are the natural learning opportunities that go unused. Students in many professional programs, for example, are required to write a great deal. Often neither the student nor the professor takes these occasions as an opportunity to improve writing skill. The focus is on content, and writing is simply a necessity. Thousands of graduate-school presentations have been made with little attention to them as opportunities to improve public speaking skill. The prevailing attitude seems to be one of survival. Both the writing and speaking in graduate classrooms may reinforce bad habits as much as or more than they improve skill; they could be made a much more effective learning opportunity. Other examples abound in the professional classroom and the workplace. Interview-like encounters occur for most of us everyday without our using them as a skill development opportunity. The need to perform some task with the computer may be a missed opportunity to learn a new routine.

## ABANDONING EXCUSES

Taking time to learn anything new or get better at something old takes time and energy. This is the reason, or excuse, many people do nothing to further develop these generic skills. For most of us, time and energy are scarce resources. At least there is more we should or would like to do than time allows—even if it is watching more football or reading more novels. For the skills discussed here, the "I don't have time" argument may be valid in the short term, but is clearly false or very weak in the long run. These skills have two payoffs when they are well developed: (1) better performance, (2) achieved with less time and energy. Part of the reason to improve writing skill, for example, is to enable us to write faster. That applies to the other skills as well.

The other point that undermines the "I don't have time" argument is that with a little forethought, natural learning opportunities can be used without taking additional time. A theme addressed throughout the book is the potential for converting routine activities into useful learning experiences, largely through the perspective with which we approach them.

We are fortunate in today's society to have many skill-development resources available. There are hundreds of books about writing, for example. There are so many learning opportunities on so many topics that they may seem overwhelming. There is need for road maps and strategies for following them. The challenge is to get a sense of the variety of skills we find useful to develop, set some priorities among them, and develop strategies for improving those skills while still doing all the other things we must do in today's often hectic life-style.

## ACKNOWLEDGMENTS

As with most books, this one was not a solitary undertaking. I owe thanks to a number of people. The most important are many career managers and professionals who have emphasized the importance of these skills for personal effectiveness and career success. That list would be long and surely incomplete, so I thank them without their names.

The idea of developing a book began to take form while I was chairing a committee on building skills into the Masters in Public Administration curriculum at Virginia Commonwealth University. Amin Alimard, Gary T. Henry, and

Marcia Lynn Whicker were members of the committee and contributed to my understanding of the importance of these skills. The interest was continued with a presentation to the Annual Conference on Teaching Public Administration and the publication of an article on the subject in a special issue of the *International Journal of Public Administration,* edited by Beverly Cigler.

The chapter on writing (chapter 2) benefitted from the ideas and suggestions of Elisabeth Brocking, C. W. Griffin, and Janice L. Thomas. Experience with Toastmasters International was an important source of information and inspiration for the chapter on public speaking (chapter 3). I also benefitted from the ideas and bibliographic assistance provided by Herbert W. Oglesby and Julia A. Walker. Virginia Cherry and Wendell Point assisted with the bibliographic work on interviewing (chapter 4). James E. Creamer provided general assistance with several parts of the book and bibliographic support for the chapter on relating. Cindy Hanchak and Marcia Lynn Whicker offered ideas and feedback on a draft of the computer chapter (chapter 6). Virginia Cherry is the lead author of the searching chapter (chapter 7). Needless to say, I claim full responsibility for any possible shortcomings of the book.

# 1

# The Pivotal Nature of Generic Skills

You can be fully knowledgeable of your profession and still be unsuccessful, sometimes for the lack of basic, generic skills.

- A military officer may know his specialty but lose his chance for impact and maybe promotion because he is unable to conduct an effective briefing.
- A physician may know her specialty thoroughly but misdiagnose because she does not know how to interview a patient.
- A government manager may have a great idea that goes nowhere because he is unable to put it into an effective written form.
- A city planner may be drowning in information but not be able to locate the critical data needed to solve a problem.
- A team leader may have the best of intentions and alienate those on whom she depends because of misunderstood behavior.
- An employee may leave an organization meeting without the information he wanted because of a fear of asking a question in a large group.
- Participants may spend hours in a meeting with the feeling that time is being wasted and nothing is getting accomplished.
- The most technically competent professional may lose a promotion because of inability to relate to co-workers.

These are just a few of the real examples of poor skills getting in the way of personal and organizational effectiveness.

## TENDENCY TO IGNORE GENERIC SKILLS

Professional and administrative education seems to focus on content to the exclusion of some of the skills essential to effective performance in the workplace. Not all of these skills are always ignored, but many professional-training programs assume that the skills are unimportant, already mastered, or will be acquired on the job. Many professionals, consequently, limp through their careers, missing some of the abilities that make the difference between success, mediocrity, and failure. Further, even if they are adequately addressed in educational programs, they, like other skills and other areas of knowledge, require continual maintenance, development, and updating. A skill is not mastered once and maintained at a high level with no attention.

Six fundamental skills are addressed in this book: writing, public speaking, interviewing, relating to others, personal computing, and information searching. These topics are tied together with an emphasis on learning as a lifetime endeavor. As these pages will indicate, there are many sources of information about each of these skills. An objective more important than providing simply a manual about each is to provide strategies for learning them—including selecting from and using the material and opportunities already available.

The tendency to ignore these basic skills is commonplace. They may seem so fundamental that no attention is given to them or no special effort is made to improve them. Writing, after all, is something we have been taught since kindergarten. "If we don't know it now, we never will" may be the prevalent attitude. Public speaking is something, it seems, we must do every now and then, although, usually, if we play our cards right, we can get out of it. So no reason to really worry about that. Interviewing? That's just talking to people. We certainly know how to talk to people. Working with other people is just a normal part of life. We don't think there is much to learn there. Maybe we should learn something about computers, but why rush? We might as well wait until they become cheaper and easier to use. Information search is something that researchers do, not us. The human mind has an extraordinary capacity to ignore what seem to be unpleasant tasks. One message intended in this book is that skill development can be an enjoyable as well as a productive process.

## THE GENERIC SKILLS IN BRIEF

### Writing

Clearly, writing is a fundamental skill. Our instruction begins in kindergarten, maybe before. Yet complaints are legion about poor writing skills in professional and organizational settings. Further, writing is a distasteful chore for many, even feared by some. Yet it is a critical part of responsibility for many professionals and managers and would be an added bonus if others did more of it. Especially with the writing tools now available, namely the computer and word processing, and current ideas about how to improve writing skill, people can make noticeable progress in both the efficiency of the writing process and the quality of the product. In many respects it is easier to improve writing skills as an established professional than as a student, although it is desirable and possible for both.

### Speaking

Public speaking is still one of those activities consistently avoided by many people, including well-established professionals and managers. The requirements and opportunities for public speaking are numerous. Not to be good at, indeed, not to enjoy it, is to waste the time of others and create unnecessary stress for ourselves. There are ready-made, low-threat learning opportunities that give professionals and managers no excuse not to become effective speakers.

### Interviewing

Interviewing is sometimes thought of as a specialized activity of personnel officers and social science researchers. Not so; it is a common and important activity of virtually everybody; it is especially common and important among managers and professionals of every kind. It is a critical source for information we use and the interactions we have. Yet, poor interviewing is as common as effective interviewing. The result is misinformation and misunderstanding. Self-directed learning in this skill is readily available.

### Relating

While writing, speaking, and interviewing are all acts of relating to others, the topic of interpersonal relations cannot be captured by those specific skills alone. Relating to others more effectively, especially in an organizational environment, is a broad concern, but skill in this area can be improved. Skill at relating, both to individuals and in groups, has an important impact on productivity and the enjoyment of professional life.

### Computing

The potential for microcomputers (as well as other varieties) in our professional and personal lives has barely been tapped partly because of new technological developments and partly because current capacity is dramatically underused. Many professionals are regular, sometimes sophisticated, users, but many have yet to touch a keyboard. The holdouts will become fewer and fewer, but the gap between potential and actual use may still increase. The learning opportunities in the microcomputer field are plentiful, so plentiful that it may seem overwhelming to the uninitiated.

## Searching

Book after book either celebrates or laments the emergence of the knowledge society. It is not the production of things that is central to modern life, it is information, the argument goes. Yet accompanying this development is information overload, or the danger of it. While an overwhelming and growing amount of information is available, the tools to manage it are on the horizon. The key is the ability to pinpoint the information needed rather than be overwhelmed by the extraordinary amount that is not. Electronic search and management of information is one of the skills the modern professional and manager needs now and will require even more in the years ahead.

## Learning

This last item does and does not belong on the skill list. It does in the sense that increasing the capacity and activity of learning does have skill components; it does not in that a major point of the chapter is to encourage the development of the habit of continuing to develop the other six skills. The emphasis is on self-directed learning, including the skill to convert an ordinary work situation into a genuine learning opportunity.

## PAYOFF

All of these fundamental skills, or the effort to improve one's ability to perform each of them, could be and often is dismissed. This is a mistake for several reasons. First, the effort to develop the skills treated here will have a payoff in efficiency. We will get all of the time back, with dividends. Not only can an effort devoted to writing skill improve the quality of the written product, it can also increase writing speed. Writing chores can be completed more quickly, leaving more time for other things. I won't say that practice at public speaking will make you speak faster—that might be counterproductive. But the preparation for it may go more quickly and the agony of anticipation may be lessened. Indeed, the agony may be replaced with a sense of excitement and positive anticipation.

Interviewing skill can remove the need to go back for more information or prevent a time-consuming error based on misinformation. Part of the point of the information search process is to pinpoint information need and source and thereby to prevent the need for time-consuming rambling searches. Computing skill clearly can be a time-saver. (It also can provide a temptation to tinker, so it is a skill that must be managed if saving time is the objective.) One of the modern professional's greatest time-wasters is poorly managed relationships. Untold hours are lost because of relationships not tended to and interactions managed poorly. Sometimes these are based in personality and emotion and sometimes they are simply a matter of "mechanics."

Effectiveness is the second reason for improving these skills. Not only will improved skill increase the speed of your writing, but hopefully, its effectiveness—the degree to which it communicates information to or persuades the reader. Writing is an important means to get other persons to take the action you wish them to take. A quality presentation may make the difference between an idea accepted or rejected. A good interview may mean the difference between hiring someone who will or someone who will not add substantially to the organization's productivity. The ability to run a meeting or manage a series of workgroup problem-solving sessions may make the difference between a decision that works and one that leads down the wrong path. Personal ability to get things done on the computer may mean the difference between showing up for a presentation with a set of high-quality, professional graphics or none at all. Information search skills may mean the difference between up-to-date or obsolete information. All of these skills have the potential for increasing both the speed and the quality of our work. They also have desirable payoffs in leisure time.

## LEISURE PAYOFF, TOO

While a primary theme is the application of these skills in a work environment, they clearly have potential for making a contribution to leisure activities. Some of these skills, public speaking for example, are themselves significant as leisure activities for many. Active membership in Toastmasters or a regular schedule of speaking engagements can be a principal form of leisure. Writing is a favorite pastime of some. And these skills may also be instrumental in making other leisure activities more accessible, meaningful, and enjoyable. Interviewing skill, in the conversational mode, may make for a much richer tour of historical sites. Writing skill and the use of a word processor may make it possible to contribute to a newsletter, or even edit one, for a leisure-oriented association. Active participants in many voluntary organizations have the opportunity to make public presentations.

These skills are a useful resource for leisure activities, and these leisure activities may provide learning opportunities to develop and hone the skills that may in turn be put to good advantage in professional life. Professional and avocational activities may be mutually reinforcing.

## PROFESSIONAL VITALITY

It is easy for a professional or manager to become stale, to get caught in a pattern of activity that begins to seem routine. The sense of forward movement that makes a professional career exciting may become minimal. "Professional vitality" suggests the possibility for continuing forward movement and excitement. The professional vitality concept is often used to suggest what organizations should do for their employees. "On the individual level, work assignments can be designed so that they stretch the professional and *cause the need* for continued learning and growth in capability" (Miller 1990: 234). The concept need not be left as something for someone else to do for you. It can be converted to an individually sought goal rather than left for others to provide for you. Of course, any opportunity to make the workplace one that stimulates professional vitality should be pursued.

Skill development can help prevent or overcome that sense of routine and assist in the achievement of professional vitality. A decision really to improve as a public speaker and then follow it up with a plan of action, for example, can inject an important spark that brings on new professional vitality. The other skills have the same potential.

## SKILL LEARNING

Skills are action-oriented. They require doing to learn, and it is through doing that the payoffs of skills are achieved. While this is a book to be read and reflected on, the bias is toward doing. Improving writing skill requires writing; public speaking skill is not developed without speaking in front of real people; computing skill requires actually sitting at the keyboard and using the computer. At the same time, a conceptual understanding of the skill and how it can be used can dramatically improve the ability to develop a skill and expand it over time. The learning of a specific technique can be improved by a broader understanding of where it fits in a larger picture—how and when it is appropriately used and for what purpose. Computing can be learned by walking through a set of commands in rote fashion. But those commands can be learned and used more effectively if you have some knowledge of how the system works. So skill development is an action-oriented process, but some knowledge of purpose and system is also important.

## Learning Through Current Activities

An idea that permeates the book is the notion that much of the learning about these (and other) skills can take place in daily activities. While you can take a week and go to a distant city for a seminar, that disruption of routine may not be necessary for learning and skill development. Being alert to learning opportunities that naturally occur may be just as important and perhaps even more powerful.

Part of being alert to learning opportunities is to avoid defining any skill too narrowly. To define public speaking, for example, as making only speeches is to lose the opportunity to practice public-speaking skills in much less threatening circumstances. An example may help make this point. Recently, I spent five hours in a project briefing. Three people sat around a table, with one person presenting information to two new project team members. Fortunately for the two of us in the "audience" the presenter exhibited many of the positive features of public speaking. A five-hour presentation in monotone would have been deadly. In fact, it was a low-threat opportunity to practice public speaking.

A more passive version of learning from current activities is to observe others in action and learn from their successes and failures. Two steps, not taken by most of us most of the time, are to evaluate the performance of others by identifying ideas and behaviors that we can adapt or that we should avoid, and at least mentally trying out how the idea would work if we used it.

## Multiplier

A real boost to skill development results from a kind of multiplier effect. A high level of skill in one area seems to make it easier to master another. One reason simply may be that skill mastery improves self-confidence, which in turn helps makes it more comfortable to take the risks involved in a new venture (Gard 1986: 9).

Beyond the self-confidence factor, further developing these skills is a mutually reinforcing activity. Improvement in one skill will make it directly or indirectly easier to develop others. Indirectly, this reinforcement comes about because the habit of skill development is transferable. Improving one skill builds a learning habit that carries over to the next.

Secondly, these skills are directly reinforcing. We often think and write about these skills as if they are discrete and separable. In fact they run together. Writing is often involved in preparing for speaking; speaking skill is a part of interviewing, both as interviewer and interviewee; all three can be components of relating; searching can be closely tied to using a computer; and using a computer can be an important tool in writing.

## Stages of Skill Development

The uncomfortable periods in developing a new skill or even dusting off and revitalizing an old one may inhibit getting started. Any skill development involves an awkward stage. Think of a physical skill you developed to a reasonable level of proficiency—perhaps diving, skiing, painting, or playing piano. You can probably recall both awkward and rewarding periods. Several years ago I took up whitewater canoeing and can vividly remember some of both moments. Now I teach canoeing classes and can observe many of the same feelings in others taking up the sport. The development of my canoeing skill involved these stages:

1. excitement about something new

2. apprehension and reluctance

3. awkward period

4. beginning to get it

5. relative comfort—a plateau

6. decision to move beyond the first plateau

7. repetition in milder form of the first four stages

8. high degree of confidence and feeling of mastery

9. recognition that there is plenty of room for improvement.

The development of the generic skills treated here runs through much the same sequence. Expecting this or a similar pattern is helpful for anticipating the less-comfortable stages and recognizing that they are temporary and for looking forward to the enjoyment of doing something with ease that once was difficult or even impossible.

## Self-Directed Learning

Most formal education for students, despite a series of fads and reforms that have made some inroads, is still "other directed." A student after a certain age may make a few big decisions, but teachers and professors make even more. Professional education is especially subject to other direction. It is not unusual for a student in a forty-five-credit-hour master's degree program to have only three or six hours of electives, if any.

Within these prescribed courses, most decisions are made for the student as well. Reading assignments are made and comprehension is tested; projects are specified, completed, and evaluated; lectures are given. It is only at the margin that students have any choice about what is important to learn or how to learn. It is easy to get in the habit of waiting to be told what is important to learn and how to learn it. Seeking out learning opportunities is not a habit cultivated by the professional educational process. One of the sub-themes in this book is encouragement to assume the attitude of a self-directed learner (Knowles 1975). Seek out learning opportunities. Don't wait for someone else to suggest attending a workshop. Don't even wait for a workshop. Take a more active stance toward identifying what is worth learning, and design ways to learn it.

### Assessing Skill Development Need

In thinking about setting a learning agenda, consider not only what you need now but also what you expect to need or would like to have in the future. Here are four categories for assessing skill development:

1. What do you do now? What are the generic skills you put to use now and how well do you perform them?

2. What additional skills or performance level would be helpful in your current position or professional situation or in your leisure activities?

3. What would be helpful or would you like to be able to do when you reach the next professional level or begin a new avocational pursuit?

4. What would be helpful or would you like to be able to do when you reach your highest professional level or in your avocational pursuits when you retire?

Grappling with these questions offers you an opportunity to give some thought to the immediate and the long-term future. Decide which skill would be most useful right now and which one will be the most useful during your career. Of the important basic skills, whether on my list or not, which is likely to have the biggest payoff during the next ten, fifteen, or twenty years? Conversely, what if you did nothing to improve your weakest skill over your career? Would it matter in terms of career success or in career enjoyment? What if you brought that skill to a high level of mastery?

## BOOK PLAN

Each of the six generic skills covered in the book is the subject of a separate chapter. Providing at least a few thoughts about the importance of the skill area is one of the tasks in each of the chapters. The intent is to offer some basis for your reflection about the use of the skill in your current as well as future circumstances.

A second feature of each chapter, sometimes interwoven with the first, is a mini "how to" manual for each skill. It is neither intended nor possible to provide comprehensive instruction here; books longer than this one have been written about each skill. It is possible, though, to provide some useful ideas as well as a sense of what else in the topic area might be worth pursuing.

The learning strategies section is the payoff feature of each chapter. It offers a series of ideas intended as stimuli for you to design your own learning approach. Many of the ideas can be adopted as presented, but they are most effective if adapted to your own situation and interest. The intent is not to provide a single path to follow. Part of the learning strategies section is a listing of other materials illustrative of what is available but not an exhaustive list. The items listed are worthy of attention, but so are others. The intent is to provide a few ideas as a stimulus to your own exploration.

## OPPORTUNITIES FOR SKILL DEVELOPMENT

One of the opportunities adults in modern society have is to improve their own knowledge and skills based on their own choices. Society is full of opportunities for learning new skills and developing new knowledge. Whether for a hobby or for a vocational skill, the resources for learning are plentiful and growing. As the chapters that follow show, providing opportunities for personal development has become a major commercial enterprise as well as a major activity of the nonprofit and public sectors. Whether you want to develop your skill at skiing, painting, selling, or home repair, there is a short course, book, videotape, or computer program waiting. Some, of course, are of high quality and some are not. Some are inexpensive and some are not.

These prepackaged, instructional opportunities are not the only way to go about building new skills or reviving old ones. Designing your own approach is equally possible and may be preferable. It is also possible to build skill development into daily routine. Skill development can be a big part or it can be a barely noticeable part of what you do every day.

Part of the effort can be to work toward creating the conditions that make learning for you and others more achievable. This may mean institutionalizing skill development. If we can talk about institutionalizing innovation (Miller 1987), doing the same with skill development should not be difficult.

This book is not about skiing, painting, selling, or home repair. It is about fundamental skills that every professional uses or could use on a regular basis. The central idea is this: there are some core skills that determine to a large degree the extent to which other knowledge and skill can be effectively put to use. Most professionals have in-depth knowledge in some area. The extent to which that knowledge is appreciated, is put to use, has an impact, or leads to success is dependent on other basic skills—the ones highlighted in this book.

These are skills for modern society. If one theme permeates the literature about contemporary society and our future, it is that we have entered a knowledge phase (Cleveland 1985, Nanus 1989, Toffler, 1990). Knowledge, not things, is the source of prestige and power. It is knowledge that allows the accumulation of power and wealth. These are skills for negotiating the turbulence and the opportunities of a knowledge society. These are among the skills that put knowledge to work for you.

## REFERENCES

Cleveland, Harlan. (1985). *The Knowledge Executive: Leadership in an Information Society*. New York: Truman Talley Books.

Gard, Grant G. (1986). *The Art of Confident Public Speaking*. Englewood Cliffs, N.J.: Prentice-Hall.

Knowles, Malcolm S. (1975). *Self-Directed Learning: A Guide for Learners and Teachers*. Chicago: Follett.

Miller, Donald Britton. (1990). "Organizational, Environmental, and Work Design Strategies That Foster Competence." In *Maintaining Professional Competence: Approaches to Career Enhancement, Vitality, and Success Throughout a Work Life*, ed. Sherry L. Willis and Samuel S. Dubin. San Francisco: Jossey-Bass.

Miller, William C. (1987). *The Creative Edge: Fostering Innovation Where You Work*. Reading, Mass.: Addison-Wesley.

Nanus, Burt. (1989). *The Leader's Edge: The Seven Keys to Leadership in a Turbulent World*. Chicago: Contemporary Books.

Toffler, Alvin. (1990). *Power Shift: Knowledge, Wealth, and Violence at the Edge of the 21st Century*. New York: Bantam Books.

# 2

## Writing: A Critical and Often Neglected Skill

The question is not whether a professional or manager needs to improve writing skills, but how much and in what ways. Virtually all of us can profit from improvement in writing. The urgency of this need can be gauged by two questions: How important is writing in what you do (and expect to do in the future)? How well do you write now? For most professionals and managers, the answer to the first question is certainly "Very important." Whether writing notes, memos, letters, reports, instructions, brochures, proposals, articles, speeches, or books, most of us write with regularity, and if it were all added up, we write a larger amount than we might think. Even if we have reached an organizational rank that affords the luxury of someone else writing for our signature, our eye for the written word is still important.

The answer to the second question, How well do you write now, varies, but the attention given the subject and the frequency of complaints about poor writing suggest that most of us have plenty of room for improvement. There really are two important parts to this question: What is the quality of your written product? How efficiently do you write? The quality of any given written document is, of course, an important measure of writing quality. The relative amount of time and effort that went into it is also important. If too much energy is devoted to a document, others of equal importance may not be written at all or other important tasks may be left undone. Writing quality definitely should be measured by both its effectiveness and its efficiency.

The thoughts about writing here do not promote a single system for writing. There are a number of books (some mentioned in the resource section below) that describe a specific approach to writing that the authors have found effective. What is effective for one person, though, may not be for another. The intent here is to stimulate you toward developing a personalized "writing system," borrowing from others as many ideas as work for you. The ultimate success is not to become a perfect writer but to develop and pursue a strategy for continuous improvement.

The suggestions about writing improvements offered here are divided into three parts:

• the writing process,

• the writing product, and

• strategies for improving both.

## THE WRITING PROCESS

When we think about improving writing skill, the first thing that comes to mind for most of us is the product—what the final document should be. Imbedded in this mental image of writing improvement are likely to be thoughts about rules of grammar, punctuation, subject-verb agreement, and the many errors that have been pointed out in our writing over the years. Product is important; without it most writing would not be done. (Although some writing might have value for the author even if the final product were destroyed.) For improving writing skill though, a valuable place to devote attention is on process. Process includes lots of things: the physical setting, the sequence of steps, the writing instruments used, the adaptation from one writing task to another, the kind of interaction with other people, the search for information, and many others.

One of the difficulties of making suggestions about writing process is that the process we use should differ from task to task. Much of the literature about writing tends to ignore it and describe writing as if it were a monolithic activity. Writing a one-paragraph handwritten note is clearly different from writing a formal memo, which is in itself different from writing a long report or a book. An effective writer will have different writing procedures depending on the task and the circumstance. And the writing process will vary even for similar tasks. A person who writes a lot may vary the process from product to product just to relieve boredom.

Similarly, writing process will vary from person to person. In tackling the same task, two equally skilled writers may go about it quite differently. The process that you and I use to write is a personal matter; there is no single system that suits everyone. That does not mean, however, that the writing process should be left to chance—without self-reflection or efforts at improvement. There is plenty we can learn from others and from trial and error. Of course, you should treat the advice given by others like a cafeteria and select only that which appeals to you, advice that applies to what is said here as well.

Ideally, writing should be effective, efficient, and, at least some of the time, fun.


### Physical Setting

Writing can be stimulating, but it is always hard work. Anything that can be done to make writing easier should be considered. Making it easier means developing a sequence that minimizes wasted motion. That, in part, means creating a physical setting conducive to writing. If getting ready to write the first word requires clearing the dining room table, collecting paper from one place, a pen from another, rearranging the light, and so on, the temptation not to start may be overwhelming. And if you do start, the need to find something else may take you in front of the TV, which happens to have a dramatic scene unfolding and . . . you get the point. Some offices also are arranged in a way that inhibits writing. Even if writing is not the main thing you do, putting things in a writing-conducive arrangement may take some of the pain out of it. Time wasted in running after supplies in an office means time not available for playing tennis, or whatever a little extra time is worth to you.

Make the physical environment attractive and inviting. By all means, make sure your chair is comfortable (for writing, not sleeping). Experiment with the word processor arrangement. The moveable keyboard makes a word processor more flexible than a typewriter, allowing some strange and comfortable writing positions.

Maintain the physical environment and the material you are working with so that you can write at any time, even if you only have a few minutes. Waiting for an adequate block of time to "really get something done" is a certain form of procrastination.

### Writing Instruments

Technology has brought us a long way since quill pens. What instrument we use to record our thoughts on paper is now one of the choices we may make. Among other possibilities, we may choose a pencil, pen, typewriter, dictaphone, secretary who takes dictation, or computer. Here and in the chapter on computing a strong case is made for using the computer to produce first drafts as well as final products. Your selection of writing instrument is an important decision. It is part of the strategy, like physical setting, to make writing easier as well as more effective. Calculate how many pages you are likely to write over the next ten years or how many hours you will spend writing. How much is a ten percent increase in efficiency worth?

*A note on writing with a computer.* The changes in communication technology over the centuries have changed the character of human relationships. It is not simply that we can communicate more quickly and over longer distances; power relationships are altered as well. Similarly, as we have moved from early written communication through paper and ink and printing press to typewriter and now computer-based word processing, the nature of writing has shifted. It is not simply that it is possible to write faster and produce perfect copies; the way the composing process takes place is also shifting. Moving from a pen (or even typewriter) to a computer as the principal drafting instrument has an impact on the thought process and sequence of composing (Daiute 1985). The impact that the widespread availability of word processors and desktop publishing systems will have is not yet clear. Experts disagree about whether using a computer improves or detracts from writing quality. My guess is that there will continue to be a steady increase in the use of word processing both for professional and personal writing, but that there will be a few holdouts and a regular subtheme of criticism and reluctant users.

For me and perhaps for you, the question is how to take advantage of the features writing with a computer offers while guarding against any negative effects on the quality of work. Here are a few things to consider and guard against. Computers can:

- produce sloppier writing.
- cause more to be written than is needed, resulting in paper overload.
- invite the overuse of boilerplate (prewritten standard text inserted in documents).

- encourage a false perfectionism in the form of too much revision.
- create a distance between writers and their words and ideas.
- encourage writers to recycle old material.

The arguments about the opportunities computers create for improving writing are equally numerous. They can:

- allow a freer, more experimental attitude about writing since revision is so much easier.
- encourage more carefully crafted products.
- free writers from the tendency toward a linear writing process and allow a more organic approach.
- minimize writer's block.
- reduce the time between first draft and final copy.

The challenge, then, is to develop the skills and habits that minimize the negative consequences and maximize the positive ones. Recognize the traps that using a computer in writing may present, but take advantage of the features that improve efficiency and effectiveness.

### Writing Sequence

There are many ways to go about writing. A writing process, no matter which of the many possibilities you use, can be divided into three parts: predrafting, drafting, and postdrafting. Even a handwritten note has some predrafting and postdrafting activity, although they may be minimal. A research manuscript may be primarily predrafting. With this simple framework in mind, let us look at a number of writing procedures. The point is not to suggest that any one is best but to put them down as a basis for evaluating and trying each one for personal fit. While reviewing these procedures think about how appropriate they might be for you and for differing tasks and circumstances. Also consider some combinations; take an idea from here and there and design your own process; work on developing a writing process that fits you.

For many products, I prefer the following writing process:

### Process 1. Craftsman
1. Think about the topic or project and jot down whatever comes to mind. Sometimes this may be a lot; sometimes a little.

2. Establish a "repository" for ideas, clippings, etc., including the ideas jotted down in step 1, and collect these as they occur.

3. Develop a rough and very changeable outline of the product.

4. Write a rough draft on the word processor.

5. Print a copy of the draft and mark it up.

6. Rewrite based on the marked-up copy. (These last two steps may be repeated several times.)

7. Let it sit for a while (depending on time available.)

8. Print a copy, mark it, and revise.

9. Get feedback. (Sometimes this leads back to step 6.)

10. Write final draft.

11. Proofread and correct. (Preferably with help from a spell-checker program and friends.)

12. Let it go.

This is a fairly extended process. Most of my writing, and I expect yours, does not have the luxury of that extended drafting period. Sometimes it is more like the second process.

### Process 2. Dash
1. Give some thought to the topic and make a mental note of the points to be covered.

2. Draft.

3. Look it over for any obvious errors.

4. Let it go.

Many other variations are possible.

### Process 3. Brainstorm Start

1. Do some solitary brainstorming, and write down, without making evaluative judgments, any idea that comes to mind.

2. Review the list and throw out any junk.

3. Reorder the list.

4. Begin drafting, using the list as an outline.

5. Draft an introduction and conclusion.

6. Revise (sometimes once, sometimes more), proof, and let it go.

### Process 4. From Impulse to Order

1. After a little thought, just start writing—mostly on impulse.

2. Using the product of the impulse writing, go back and develop an outline, reordering, discarding, and so forth.

3. Rewrite, based on the outline.

4. Revise, proof, and let it go.

### Process 5. Incremental Outlining

1. Develop a broad-brush outline.

2. Outline one section and then draft it.

3. Outline the next section, then draft it, and so on.

4. Revise (extensive or minimal), proof, and let it go.

### Process 6. Boilerplate Writing

1. Develop an approach.

2. Write some and insert a prewritten boilerplate section.

3. Write another sentence or so and insert boilerplate.

4. Proof the transitions and printing quality and let it go.

### Process 7. Argument-Tree Approach

1. Think through the needs of the audience.

2. Analyze the problem and its solution using a tree structure.

3. Using the tree structure as an outline, draft.

4. Revise, proof, and let it go (adapted from Holcombe and Stein 1987).

### Process 8. Throw It Away and Restart

1. Develop a stream-of-consciousness draft.

2. Review the draft and throw it away.

3. Develop a new draft.

Writing sequence does matter, but there is no single right way for every writer or for every occasion. Writing jointly with someone else also can alter the process. Coauthorship deserves some attention before the drafting process begins. At least some minimal agreement about responsibilities, format, and sequence can help keep coauthors on friendly terms and make the working relationship productive.

### Tips for Getting Started and Curing Writer's Block

Strategies for the times that words do not flow should be part of any good writing process. You are sitting with pen and paper or word processor, and the ideas and words not only don't flow, they don't even make an appearance. Besides giving up and going out for a beer, what can you do? Here are a few thoughts: some of them I've used and others have been culled from literature or suggested by others.

Sometimes just starting is the toughest. After a beginning things pick up, and in an hour or so it begins to be engaging. So the key is to get started (no different from jogging, except that for some persons jogging never becomes engaging). What are some tricks?

• Just turn on the machine. I have found that I am more likely to write if the word processor in my office already is turned on. Somehow a cold monitor is an inhibitor. So the first thing I do when I go into my office now is turn the computer on (it won't hurt it). If an idea comes along, I am then more likely to enter it, and if I write the first sentence, others are more likely to follow.

• Before going home at night, decide what the writing starting point is for the next day and lay out the material needed for it. Put it right in the middle of your desk so it cannot be ignored.

• Bribe your brain. Say: "After I get the first paragraph written, I will get a cup of coffee." (Not "I will get started after I get a cup of coffee." Candy bars also work well, but have certain undesirable side effects.)

• You may think of other get-started strategies that are more effective for you.

You have gotten to the desk or the word processor and have tried to write. Nothing is happening. Your mind is blank, and it feels like there is a wall between you and the words you want to see on the screen.

• Burst writing (Sullivan et al. 1989: 58) is one technique that sometimes helps get over the wall. Just write anything about the subject; or, if necessary, about anything at all. Getting words to start flowing to the screen can be enough to overcome the barrier.

• Invisible writing involves turning the light down on the monitor and starting writing without being able to see the words (Sullivan et al. 1989: 122). The idea is based on the notion that seeing the words is sometimes an inhibitor. Seeing the words causes the writer to stop and evaluate what has been written, the evaluation turns out negative, and so writing stops.

• Individual brainstorming may get the creative juices flowing. Write down as many ideas as you can think of without evaluating them. Keep it up as long as new ideas come, even through a lull or two. Just as in group brainstorming, a five-minute warm-up period on a topic unrelated to what you intend to write about may be useful.

• Write about the topic from a radically different perspective. What would a five-year-old child say about the budget crisis, or a frontiersman about the market prospects for a new dental office? In addition to getting some words flowing, the hypothetical five-year-old or frontiersman may have a good idea or two that you can use.

• As difficult as it sometimes is to admit, the problem may be that you have nothing to say or have not decided how to handle the situation about which you are writing. More reading, research, and thinking may be the only effective way through the barrier.

There is plenty of room for creativity in designing the writing process in general and for overcoming the getting-started and writer's-block problems. You may have some favorites of your own, and the people around you may have some good ideas.

### A Note on Writing Fast

One of the frustrating things about writing is that it takes time. Although there may be a trade-off between amount of time and quality of product, spending more time does not always mean creating a superior product. I expect that if we could keep the quality of a product high, all of us would like to write faster. In thinking about this topic, I asked one of my colleagues, Marcia Lynn Whicker, known for her ability to write large amounts quickly, to give me her advice about how to do it. The following is what she wrote.

\*    \*    \*    \*    \*

The good thing about writing fast is that the more you do it the faster you get, and the faster you get, the more you do. In short, speed and volume are positively related to each other in writing, and to quality as well. People who write a lot usually are faster at it *and* better at it than are people who write intermittently and infrequently. Since writing effectively has a large skill component, those who practice their skills usually are better and faster than those who don't.

Three major impediments undermine fast writing: sloppy thinking, inadequate physical writing skills, and perfectionism and fear of criticism.

*Sloppy thinking.* Writing is nothing but thinking, crystallized and articulated. The best writers in the world are among the best thinkers. Fast writing is highly correlated with fast thinking. But just thinking quickly is insufficient for writing rapidly. High-volume producers must also think well. If you are having difficulty writing rapidly, and every sentence is torturously extracted, most likely this exhausting exertion is occurring because you have not thought through where you want to go. If you do not know where you want your chain of logic (and most good writing is a chain of logic) to end up, how can you possibly take a reader there? Each step is halting and uncertain. You cannot quickly identify the major points you want to make because you do not yet know what they are. You cannot write rapidly about something you have not yet figured out.

Inadequate "legwork" or "homework" prior to writing is one, but not the only, reason you may not know what to say. Perhaps you are writing about a topic that requires research, investigation, and the collection of information. Perhaps you have not done that adequately because collecting, absorbing, and synthesizing information is hard work. So no wonder when it comes time to write the report, you have little to say. You are like a car trying to go somewhere without adequate directions, a map, or even a full tank of gas.

By contrast, if you have read and thought enough about your topic to know the important points you wish to make, and if you have supporting and illustrative detail, then the words will flow easily. At times they may seem even to gush, and you, the writer, just shape the flow. So, the first factor in being a quick writer is having something interesting and meaningful to say.

*Inadequate physical writing skills.* Writing is like a sport. If you want to play the game, you must acquire the basic skills a fast efficient writer needs. Using a state of the art computer/word processor is one of those basic skills. You can be an adequate writer using other methods, and maybe a good one—Thomas Jefferson did write the Declaration of Independence with a quill pen—but you cannot be a fast one. And rest assured that if Jefferson, the inventor and innovator, were working today, he would have turned out "We hold these truths to be self evident" in WordPerfect 5.1. Writing fast and not using a computer are incompatible. Writing by longhand is equivalent to digging a ditch with a shovel when a backhoe is sitting nearby. Only for small ditches where the backhoe is too big to maneuver or where starting the backhoe takes longer than digging the hole . . . only for such small projects is the longhand method faster.

The other major tool a fast writer needs is a big vocabulary. Everything else being equal, which, of course, it rarely is, fast writers have big vocabularics. Numerous words pop into their mind—drawn from a large reservoir of choices.

Thus, if you want to develop rapid writing skills, become proficient with word processor and expand your vocabulary. Good writing has a richness to it that is varied, textural, and alternately subtle and bold. That richness makes writing interesting to the author as well as the reader, and the author—you—are motivated and excited and can work faster than if you were bored, repetitive, and dull.

*Perfectionism and fear of criticism.* Fast writers often do not care what others think. They are not writing because they care what others think; they are writing to tell others what to think. They are more concerned with stimulating and motivating others than they are about being criticized. Of course, they get criticized. Since persuading their readers is more important than currying their affection, criticism is hurtful, but not devastating. Perfectionism is also fear of criticism—criticism by yourself. You are afraid you will not meet your own high standards. But underlying perfectionism is a deeper fear of being criticized by others. Perfectionists just try to beat others to the punch.

Fast writers cannot sit around and worry that someone may not like them or their writing. They know before writing that probably someone won't. But they also know that life goes on, even after criticism—and so does writing. Seasoned writers know how to tell which criticisms are off the mark—motivated more by the needs and problems of the critic than by the problems of the writing product. They discount their criticisms, focus on the more valid suggestions, and go on.

*       *       *       *       *

## Process Fundamentals

A whole range of process ideas have been suggested. Some you may find helpful, and others you will discard. Despite the variation in the writing sequences, certain fundamental ideas about writing process stand out. Here are some.

*Process Fundamental 1.* Start "writing" with a file-folder, a box, a drawer, a shelf, or a computer file.

For those who follow this suggestion, much of the work of writing (or preparing a speech) is done before the drafting is started. Decide early on the general topic and then jot down any idea or information source—like a book title—or clip any related information and drop it into a "repository" during the normal course of things. It is surprising how frequently relevant ideas pop up if the basic topic has been defined and is in mind. Having a folder full of potentially usable items is a tremendous help in avoiding the writer's worst nightmare: a blank sheet of paper, a short deadline, and not even the first idea.

Beginning the actual planning and drafting process can be a real pleasure when the file folder is filled with ideas and information. I am very appreciative of the person (whose identity I can no longer remember) who first made me aware of this idea. It has made numerous tasks, some large and some small, much easier.

*Process Fundamental 2.* Write so that revision is easy. And then revise.

Making it easy to revise contributes to a quality product in two ways. First, if it is easy to revise, the writer is not as likely to let a shoddy piece of work pass for a final product. The harder it is to revise, the greater is the temptation to decide that making changes is not worth the effort. Is it, for example, worth retyping a whole page to change one word? Second, knowing that revision is easy encourages the words to flow, making the process of writing more productive. If the words put down are thought to be permanent, with no possibility of change, the writer is likely to exercise great caution and perhaps stop putting words down altogether.

Following this suggestion to make revision easy will involve different strategies for different people. For more and more writers this means drafting on a word processor. Almost without exception a writer who has learned to use a word processor is a true convert, even a zealot. Few can imagine going back to composing on a typewriter or in longhand. Ease of revision is a major reason for this commitment. (An added bonus of a word processor is instant

gratification, or at least speedier gratification. A clean looking product is available much faster.)

Not knowing how to type is a roadblock many people
face in learning word processing. Developing rudimentary
typing skills will be well rewarded. Use the word processor
to learn typing; errors are forgiven more easily on a screen
than on a typewriter, and typing instruction programs are
available in computer packages.

For the writer who is not ready for the transition to a
word processor, making revision easy may involve other
techniques. For the longhand writer, a shift to drafting by
writing on every other line and on only one side of the paper
may make a big difference in the ease of revision. This allows "cutting and pasting" and insertions. Drafting single
space on both sides of the paper makes revision difficult.
There are other approaches; the point is to take down the
barriers to rewriting however you can.

A corollary to the suggestion to make revision easy is:
"Get it down now, get it right later."

Making it easy to revise is a big part of the battle, but the
revision still has to be done. It does not occur by itself, and
it may still be painful. Encouragement to endure the pain of
rewriting is provided by Ernest Hemingway:

> *Interviewer:* How much rewriting do you do?
> *Hemingway:* It depends. I rewrote the ending of *A Farewell to
> Arms* . . . thirty-nine times before I was satisfied.
> *Interviewer:* Was there some technical problem there? What was
> it that had you stumped?
> *Hemingway:* Getting the words right. [quoted in Trimble 1975:
> 95]

*Process Fundamental 3.* Get feedback.

There is a strong tendency to make writing a solitary activity. Certainly most of our schooling treated writing as an
individual undertaking. Those of us who have tried to "write

by committee," with each word and comma subject to debate and group consensus, might argue that writing should be solitary. But a writing process can profit greatly from the participation of others. That participation can take a variety of forms and be brought in at many stages in the process.

For some people, asking for critical comments and suggestions is the most difficult part of the writing process; for others, it's the most enjoyable. The specific steps in getting feedback depend on circumstances: whether the writer is a student in a class with others doing similar assignments, is in a professional environment that has a built-in feedback process as many research organizations do, or has access to a "writing center" that offers feedback as a service. Electronic mail now provides a convenient means to give and receive feedback between people in the same building or at opposite ends of the world.

Who we should ask for feedback is an important question. The ideal person(s) is one who is supportive but who will give insightful and honest reactions. A reciprocal relationship—perhaps a "buddy system"—is probably best. (A spouse or significant other can sometimes be a good source of feedback, but not always. For some people, criticism is not well received from a source so close, and so the writing and the relationship may both suffer.)

When to get feedback is also a relevant concern. The tendency in many quarters is to wait until the next-to-last draft is completed. The idea is that by that stage the product is good enough that one's ego will not be too badly damaged, but there is still an opportunity to use any suggestions given. The danger is that we may already be defensive about what we have written. That attitude often shows through, and so the reader soft-pedals criticism that might be warranted and useful. When possible, very early feedback may be desirable. Very early may well mean the predrafting stage when the ideas are still being formed. Get some reactions before the first word is written. Maybe the central theme itself should be changed; perhaps some feedback will suggest (or stimulate you to think of) a different perspective on the topic.

*Process Fundamental 4.* Sooner or later let it go.

Sometimes there is a tendency to want a document or manuscript to be perfect, and consequently never to finish. While sloppy work is by no means recommended, it should also be recognized that perfection is never achieved. Somewhere between sloppy and perfect, stop!

Aside from controlling the urge for perfection, several ideas can be helpful in completing a writing task. One is not to be unrealistically ambitious about the product you expect to produce. If you plan a fully comprehensive report, for example, that will require more time and effort than available, the final result may be a decision not to produce the report at all or a last-minute reduction in scale without the time to develop a quality product of limited scale.

Another aid in completing a writing task is a deadline. Nothing is more effective than a real deadline for increasing the rate of word flow.

## WRITTEN PRODUCT

The purpose of the writing process is to produce efficiently a product that accomplishes its objective. Since written products are so varied—ranging from a short note to a book or more—generalizing in a few pages about an effective product is difficult. Many features are potentially worthy of comment and the attention of any writer: appearance, substance, flow, readability, tone, and more.

Several fundamental ideas stand out.

*Product Fundamental 1.* Make it easy for your audience.

Most readers have a very powerful option—they can refuse to read what we have written. If enough people exercise that option, we may as well not have written at all.

A lot of advice is available about making the written word intelligible to readers: write to the level of the audience, be direct, use the smallest word that will do the job, and so forth. Seek out such advice from books or wherever it is available and use it if it fits; much of it is well worth heeding. Here are a few ways to make writing easy for the reader that I think are especially important in professional and organizational settings.

*Subheadings.* A device for making a document easy for readers is the subheading, which provides a kind of map for the reader, a means to keep track of where one has been, where one is going, and a way to take shortcuts. In professional writing, many readers do not wish to start at the beginning and read straight through. Subheadings, among other devices, allow the reader to skim effectively, stopping to read carefully where interest warrants. Subheadings also can be a great aid to the writer, giving a picture of structure much clearer than would otherwise be possible.

Use subheadings in memoranda and even letters. Any document longer than a page or two is a candidate for some system of reader guidance. Subheadings are often the most effective.

*Bullets.* Bullets and other listing formats seem to be gaining in popularity in government, business, and other organizational documents. They offer a reader a chance to see the main points without superfluous words. Even an occasional book is now written primarily in bullet form (Dunckel and Parnham 1985). Of course the list format is not appropriate for all, or even most, products. Some of the words left out are critical to understanding. A bullet or list format can be used in many documents as an organizing feature. When it works, a large amount of information can be highlighted and conveyed efficiently.

*White space and visuals.* Some documents seem to be prepared with the primary objective of saving paper. Paper may be saved, but often at the expense of the reader's eyes and, ultimately, attention. Liberal use of blank space and other thoughtful formatting can do a lot to make it easy on a reader.

Visuals make the life of a reader easier in two ways, assuming of course that they are used appropriately. First, they perform the same function as white space by providing relief from the sameness of continuous text. Second, graphs, tables, sketches, models, and other nontext forms present information in a different way. The duplication itself can be helpful, and it takes advantage of the fact that different readers prefer different media. Some can comprehend visually presented material more easily than text.

*Summaries.* In some settings, an expected feature of a written report is an executive summary. Whether expected or not, some type of summary is one way to make your written product easy for your audience. As much as we might like for them to, most readers do not consider our written memos and reports as works of art to be devoured word for word. A more typical reaction is to want to get through it as quickly as possible and still comprehend that which is necessary to know. If the effort appears to be greater than the payoff, it won't be read. So even a summary needs to be carefully constructed with the "semi-interested" reader in mind. Ideally, a good executive summary will provide the reader with a sense of the main points in the longer document and provide some enticement to read beyond the summary. Your own judgment and artistic flair is called for, but a few points are worth considering:

- Position a summary first, or at least very early, in a report.

- Keep it brief. The sometimes-touted one-page rule should be an absolute constraint only if your boss is set on it. One page may or may not get the job done. If it can, one page is better than two, and two is better than three. By all means, do not fall into the trap of compressing the text or reducing the font size so there is no white space.

- Avoid methodology in most summaries. Occasionally it may be necessary or appropriate, but usually it tells the reader to tune out.
- Format so that key points—findings, conclusions, recommendations—stand out.
- Organize the summary to parallel the main report. This makes it easier for the reader who is enticed to read more than the summary.

Whatever the devices—those mentioned above, or a table of contents, an index, or just clear writing—make it easy for the reader. Even better, make the reader want to read what you have written.

*Product Fundamental 2.* Recognize that style appropriately differs from one document to the next.

Make sure the style matches both the situation and the desired impression. For example, in some writing, including some professional products, the use of "I" is quite appropriate. In other situations, including many administrative documents, it is not the desired form. Some pieces have a directive tone, and others are gently suggestive. Some are purposely neutral with the ring of objectivity; some are documents of advocacy. And there are other distinctions. One recent book on technical writing, for example Beason and Williams 1990, divides style into formal, semiformal, and informal. Although there is a place for all three styles, these authors suggest that semiformal is most frequently appropriate for professional and organizational writing.

The wrong style and tone can be as damaging as incorrect content, and appropriate style and tone add considerably to the effectiveness of writing.

*Product Fundamental 3.* Have a beginning, a middle, and an end.

A beginning should give the reader the context, the purpose, of the product. The reader should be able to tell almost instantly what the theme of the document is and be able to make a rapid judgment about whether it will be useful to read it.

Good writing asserts and demonstrates, tells and shows. The middle in most cases should be heavy on demonstration with clearly presented information that enables the reader to evaluate what is being said. The document should have a coherence, a clear sequence of thought. It should flow from beginning to end with a logic that carries from one idea to the next.

And the document should not just end. Some means to announce smoothly that the job is done is important to the reader. This announcement may be in the form of a summary, an effort to tie the major themes together, or a set of conclusions drawn from the work.

*Product Fundamental 4.* Make sure the product is accurate, with no typographical or other errors.

After the labor of writing, there may be a tendency to want to be done with the product, whether it is a memorandum, a brochure, a letter, a report, or any other document managers and professionals produce. The temptation is to give minimal attention to the proofreading stage, allowing fatigue or impatience or the press of other events to blind one to its importance. A final document with errors is likely to embarrass the author and other members of an organization as well as reduce the effectiveness of the product, no matter how much effort went into its development. Listen to one author on writing:

Your object is to court your reader, not alienate him. If you give him a carelessly proofread paper, you hazard his concluding at least one of these opinions about you: (a) you are an undisciplined, lazy individual; (b) you probably will be found to be as grubbyminded a thinker as you are a proofreader; and (c) you are the kind of writer whom it's going to be pure drudgery to read. It may be unjust, I agree, but it's reality. (Trimble 1975: 96)

## SELF-DIRECTED IMPROVEMENT STRATEGIES

More than one strategy to continue the improvement of writing is available. Several ideas and resources are suggested here. They are intended to be ideas you can consider and, if they fit, pick up and use. They are also meant to spark ideas of your own. As you read through them, think about specific ways you might use the suggestions as well as other ideas that you might try.

### Books

A lot has been written about how to write. Writers, like people in other fields, write about what they do. Perhaps writers do so doubly since they are writing about what they do and doing what they do. Consequently, a good deal of material is available about how to write and how to improve writing. Using such material is one strategy that can be part of a self-directed learning program.

The undergraduate composition class is the target audience for many of the books on writing, but quite a few are targeted at professionals and don't necessarily pass over those for composition students. After getting past the "how to select a topic for your essay" section, these books contain a lot of useful information and ideas. Many of the books on writing are quite short, while others are mammoth. Each has its advantages. Below are a few suggestions. The list can easily be expanded by a trip to a library or bookstore:

Beason, Pamela S., and Patricia A. Williams. (1990). *Technical Writing for Business and Industry*. Glenview, Ill.: Scott, Foresman. A detailed primer on preparing documents in professional and organizational settings.

Daiute, Colette. (1985). *Writing and Computers*. Reading, Mass.: Addison-Wesley. An extensive discussion of the writing process using a word processor. The book emphasizes teaching writing in a school setting, but much of the text is relevant to any writing setting.

Gunning, Robert, and Douglas Mueller. (1981). *How to Take the Fog Out of Writing*. The Dartnell Corporation. Part one of this booklet describes and shows how to use the Fog Index to assess the readability of prose. The remainder of the booklet provides writing guidance in the form of twenty-five common faults in professional writing and a suggested cure for each. Included are faults like "institution-itis," "pompous phrases," "lack of variety," and "passive writing."

Holcombe, Marya W., and Judith K. Stein. (1987). *Writing for Decision Makers: Memos and Reports with a Competitive Edge*. 2d ed. New York: Van Nostrand Reinhold. Gives attention to writing quickly as well as effectively. The central feature is a process for thinking through the logic of an argument before beginning to write. A tree diagram is used to show the structure of a memo or report before writing the first draft.

Holtz, Herman. (1986). *The Consultant's Guide to Proposal Writing: How to Satisfy Your Clients and Double Your Income*. New York: John Wiley & Sons. Provides a detailed guide to the specific task of writing proposals.

Hull, Raymond. (1981). *How to Write "How-To" Books and Articles*. Cincinnati, Ohio: Writer's Digest Books. A manual for hobbyists and others who want to write and publish "how-to" books, articles, and handbooks in their area of interest and expertise.

Kane, Thomas S. (1983). *The Oxford Guide to Writing: A Rhetoric and Handbook for College Students*. New York: Oxford University Press. A comprehensive book that falls in the mammoth category (820 pages). This guide treats a long list of topics about writing; it is best used as a reference.

Kaye, Sanford. (1989). *Writing Under Pressure: The Quick Writing Process*. New York: Oxford University Press. This book recognizes that much of the writing we do is required, has a time deadline, and is not the writing we would do if we could choose. In this context, the book develops and demonstrates a process for writing that emphasizes the writer's commitment and the need for few wasted motions. The chapters on writing in an organizational setting are particularly appropriate for many professionals.

Lanham, Richard A. (1979). *Revising Prose*. New York: Charles Scribner's Sons. The focus of the book is revision, especially the revision of various "bureaucratic, social-scientific, computer-engineering, military" dialects into plain English.

Monroe, Judson. (1980). *Effective Research and Report Writing in Government*. New York: McGraw-Hill. Focuses specifically on the kind of writing administrators and analysts do. Includes ideas about data collection and interpretation and other parts of the analytic and report-writing process.

Moore, Nick, and Martin Hesp. (1985). *The Basics of Writing Reports Etcetera*. London: Clive Bingley. Provides guidance in writing reports of several types: annual, research, minutes, brochures, and others. It includes a chapter on presenting statistical information.

Runkel, Philip J., and Margaret Runkel (1984). *A Guide to Usage for Writers and Students in the Social Sciences*. Totowa, N.J.: Rowman & Allanheld. A compilation of commonly misused words in social science writing. Their meanings, along with a few stylistic, punctuation, and grammatical points are offered. Examples are confusion between *adapt, adopt* and *affect, effect* and the misuse of words such as *feedback* and *interface*.

Strunk, William, Jr., and E. B. White. (1979). *The Elements of Style*. 3d ed. New York: Macmillan. A classic guide to clear writing. This brief book includes advice about common problems in punctuation, grammar, composition, and style.

Sullivan, David, J. Wesley Sullivan, and William L. Sullivan. (1989).

*Desktop Publishing: Writing and Publishing in the Computer Age.* Boston: Houghton Mifflin. Includes an introduction to the technical side of desktop publishing and word processing along with a good deal of material about the process of writing itself.

Trimble, John R. (1975). *Writing and Style: Conversations on the Art of Writing.* Englewood Cliffs, N.J.: Prentice-Hall. A readable and entertaining book written with an emphasis on literary criticism for undergraduate students. Nevertheless, it is a book most professionals would enjoy and learn from. The discussion of the writing process and the debunking of many of the rules of formal English are especially interesting chapters.

Westheimer, Patricia H. (1989). *Power Writing for Executive Women.* Glenview, Ill.: Scott, Foresman. Argues that women need to write more assertively and provides guidelines for doing so.

Zinsser, William. (1985). *On Writing Well: An Informal Guide to Writing Nonfiction.* 3d ed. New York: Harper & Row. A lively and informative book of advice on writing. It treats such topics as "clutter," "style," "the audience," and others along with chapters on "Science Writing and Technical Writing" and "Writing in Your Job."

These books can be used in several ways. One, of course, is just to peruse and dwell on particularly useful, interesting, or entertaining items. Another is to select a book and work through it carefully as a text. And some books can be very valuable as references. Don't stop with this list. New books on the topic appear regularly.

### Magazine and Journal Articles

Writing is a regular topic for articles in popular and trade magazines. Airline magazines, for example, are likely to have occasional articles on writing. Computer magazines are not only a source for information about the technical side of word processing but also occasionally provide articles with tips about the drafting or revising process itself. If you are alert for them they are likely to appear in a variety of places.

### Classes/Workshops

In many communities, systematic writing instruction is available in both credit and noncredit courses, and many organizations have periodic employee workshops. Courses and workshops may focus on creative writing for aspiring (or already successful) poets and novelists or on business and professional writing.

### Feedback

Getting regular feedback on your own writing is an important source of improvement. It can be sought from friends or work associates or from more-formal sources like a writing center. Sending materials for professional publication is also a source of feedback, sometimes good and sometimes painful.

As discussed in the section on writing process, feedback need not be at the end of the writing process. Some of the most useful reactions may come in the early stages, even in the idea stage.

One way to think about writing feedback is to treat it as helpful with the particular product in preparation. As a skill development strategy, it is useful to seek and use feedback in a more general way. Consciously use it as a source of guidance about areas to improve, techniques that can be used in future work, and so forth. Simply having somebody help fix the punctuation and grammar on a draft is useful, but does not necessarily translate into your own skill improvement.

## Writing Centers and Grammar Hotlines

The writing centers at many community colleges, colleges, and universities are potential resources. Many were originally remedial centers, but the trend is toward providing writing assistance to good writers as well as those with special problems. Some of these centers have grammar hotlines with persons available, usually during specified hours, to answer writing questions. Like feedback in general, the writing center can be treated as a resource of quick help for a particular document or as part of an overall skill development effort.

## Providing Feedback to Others

Receiving feedback from others is an important learning strategy, but so is giving feedback. Reviewing others' work to offer suggestions can be highly instructive for the evaluator. Both ideas to emulate and others to avoid may be found. Part of your skill development strategy may be to position yourself so others seek your reactions to their written work. Being asked for reactions a second and third time is likely to require you to provide helpful, not patsy, feedback, but avoid the temptation to be an ego crusher. Don't inflate your own ego at the expense of another's unless you want your tenure as a sought-out source of feedback to be short lived.

## Reading for Writing Improvement

The least disruptive opportunity for writing practice in a busy schedule is simply to notice the style and quality of what one is reading. This may include memos, letters, reports; journal articles, manuals, texts; and even novels, labels, and directions on how to operate a VCR. Here too, the key is alertness to ideas to try and ideas to avoid in your own work.

### Everyday Practice

Another means of improving skills in writing that is not time consuming or disruptive is to give attention to normal writing tasks that are already required. Give thought to how a memo or a report could be improved and use these normal writing tasks to experiment with new techniques.

### Creating Practice Opportunities

Beyond what is normally written, you may want to add some writing tasks just for the purpose of experimentation and writing improvement. Opportunities are plentiful:

- letters "above and beyond the call of duty,"
- a journal or diary with regular entries,
- efforts at short stories or other fiction,
- summaries of meetings,
- summaries of the main idea of articles, books, or reports,
- contributions to professional and avocational newsletters,
- and more.

### Experiment/Push Yourself in Small Steps

To move your writing skill ahead, push yourself. Try writing a type of document you have not done before. Experiment with a different approach. Before or after you have received feedback, you can always throw it out.

### Motivations for Writing

Develop incentives to write by creating the opportunity for writing along with the expectation that writing be done. This could include:

- participating in writing contests,
- submitting proposals to conferences and editors;

this then creates the obligation to write and a deadline,

- rewriting the same content for different audiences,

thus requiring practice at targeting presentations to specific audiences,

- developing a reputation and self-image as "a writer,"

thereby creating a self-fulfilling prophecy.

### Self-Feedback

Self-conscious practice implies that the writer is evaluating the product—providing self-feedback. Recognizing the good and the bad in any writing is not necessarily easy; it can be especially difficult in one's own writing. Here are a few questions that may help—although not equally relevant in every situation—and that may also be used when providing feedback to someone else.

1. Is the purpose clearly stated early in the document? Can the reader determine right away whether this is a useful document to read?
2. Is the style and tone appropriate for the purpose and audience of the document?
3. Is the purpose of the document accomplished?
4. Do the argument and evidence adequately support the position taken?
5. Is there a logical progression from beginning to end?
6. Are there adequate subheadings or other means to give the reader a clear map of where the document is going?

7. Is the document free of grammatical, spelling, and other errors?

8. Is the writing interesting?

## A FEW IDEAS FOR THE INHIBITED WRITER

Although there may not be as much said about fear of writing as there is of public speaking or using computers, there nevertheless are people for whom the prospect of writing, especially anything more than a note or short memo, is frightening. How might such people warm up to writing and overcome inhibitions enough to work earnestly on improving writing skill?

Making a list or inventory of the items you now write can be a useful beginning point. Include both professional and nonprofessional writing. Consciously use these as a laboratory for practice to reinforce and improve your writing skill and confidence. Additionally do some totally nonthreatening writing, writing not intended for sharing with anyone. Either with pen and paper or a computer, write about things you are very familiar with, a hobby or interest, for example. A source of advice outside the workplace can also be useful in getting comfortable with extended writing. A writing center at a college or a composition course at a community college may serve this purpose. The important step is to find some nonthreatening outlet for writing and then spend some time practicing it.

## CONCLUSION

The ideas presented here for developing a self-directed strategy for improving writing skill by no means exhaust the possibilities. The key to using these and other ideas is to build a personally tailored strategy, not to adopt someone else's suggestions without question. Writing and learning how to write more effectively are ultimately matters of personal style. However, deciding whether to work on the improvement of writing skill should be more than a matter of personal whim. The importance of writing for managers and professionals is so great that it is closer to a responsibility than a personal preference.

## REFERENCES

Beason, Pamela S., and Patricia A. Williams. (1990). *Technical Writing for Business and Industry.* Glenview, Ill.: Scott, Foresman.

Daiute, Colette. (1985). *Writing and Computers.* Reading, Mass.: Addison-Wesley.

Dunckel, Jacqueline, and Elizabeth Parnham. (1985). *The Business Guide to Effective Speaking.* London: Kogan Page.

Holcombe, Marya W., and Judith K. Stein. (1987). *Writing for Decision Makers: Memos and Reports with a Competitive Edge.* 2d ed. New York: Van Nostrand Reinhold.

Sullivan, David, J. Wesley Sullivan, and William L. Sullivan. (1989). *Desktop Publishing: Writing and Publishing in the Computer Age.* Boston: Houghton Mifflin.

Trimble, John R. (1975). *Writing and Style: Conversations on the Art of Writing.* Englewood Cliffs, N.J.: Prentice-Hall.

# 3

---

# Speaking: A Needlessly
# Feared Activity

In the midst of the high school football season my junior year, one of the players suddenly quit school and joined the army. Not until several years later did I learn why. It had been Mike's turn the following week to be game captain, and part of the game captain's responsibility was to say a few words at the pep rally. The prospect of speaking before the student body was so frightening that he preferred to drop out of school and join the army. He decided it was a fear he did not want to live with, though. After his army tour he went to acting school. The last time I saw him he was working as a professional actor.

Most people do not have a fear of public speaking strong enough to interrupt schooling or careers—at least in such dramatic fashion. But in fact many do allow fear of public speaking to interrupt or slow down their careers. They do so by passing up opportunities for speaking and by performing poorly when the occasion cannot be avoided. Not only is the opportunity to make a good impression lost, but so may be the chance to communicate important information or make a persuasive case. Public speaking in many respects parallels writing as an important professional skill. Professionals and managers are consistently called upon or have the opportunity to speak to groups. Whether this is two or three persons (one, for that matter) in an informal committee meeting or hundreds in a formal speech or briefing, comfort and skill in speaking publicly has benefits. Stories from the military, business, and politics are plentiful about persons who have made important career advances after a quality presentation, and equally plentiful about persons who have ruined promotion opportunities because of a poor performance (Leech 1982: 6).

## MULTIPLE TYPES AND OCCASIONS

Public speaking usually conjures the image of someone standing in front of an audience. That, of course, is the way much public speaking does occur. Many public speaking occasions, however, are not that way at all. One of the reasons for the fear of public speaking is the sense that it is dramatically different from the activities we perform on a more regular basis, activities with which we are familiar and therefore comfortable. If we are fully aware of the many occasions that we in fact engage in public speaking, or at least have many of the elements of public speaking, we begin to realize that it is a familiar activity. This realization also then provides many opportunities for learning and practice. The following is a small sample of activities that have many or all of the elements of public speaking:

- a session at a small conference table in which you are briefing one (or more) new employees about your part of the organization. (If you think public speaking skill is not called for in a one-on-one briefing, try being the "audience" of one for several hours.)
- the beginning meeting of a new task force in which each person is asked to introduce himself or herself.
- your role as chair of a committee.
- asking a question in a class, meeting, or presentation.

• a lunch with two or three co-workers during which you are asked to explain something.

These and many other occasions are public speaking events, but they do not have the threat of a large audience assembled especially to hear you speak. After practicing in these other low-threat situations, the large audience may be less troublesome. This is a point at the heart of the skill-development approach advocated here and practiced successfully in many settings. Develop and practice a skill in a low-threat situation. Use the low-threat environment to build confidence and hone skill. The big event is then only a small progression from where you have been. This is the strategy Toastmasters uses with public speaking; it is the strategy whitewater boating instructors use; and it is the strategy of successful boxing managers. Everyday activities can provide opportunities for this progression from a low- to high-threat performance environment.

### Types of Public Speaking

Public speaking generally falls into four major categories, but the four may not exhaust the possibilities:

Speeches

Briefings and Presentations
  Individual
  Team

Meetings

Interviews

Each has its own characteristics and nuances. Skill at one is helpful in another, but adaptation is required. Becoming a good after-dinner speaker will definitely provide some useful skills for doing briefings, but other skills are required. A good after-dinner speaker may not be very good at briefings. Some good event speakers are poor in interactive settings. President Reagan was better at prepared speaking events than in the exchange of press conferences, and so are many others.

## FOUR KEY DIMENSIONS

The four public speaking roles are different primarily in terms of four dimensions: degree of formality, degree of preparation required, degree of interaction, and amount and variety of props and audiovisual materials. The dimension often thought to be most important, size of audience, is relevant only as a function of these four. (Not as one speaker nearing the appointed day revealed, "How many people will be there? I need to know how nervous to be.")

### Formality

One of my college professors used to enter the classroom, take off his jacket, loosen his tie, and sit on the desk with his legs folded yoga-style. In fact, he was an effective teacher, whether because of or in spite of this degree of informality, I'm not sure. But his informal style would have been out of place and would have reduced his effectiveness in a presidential address to the nation, a briefing of the corporate board of directors, or even a lunchtime speech to the Lions Club. Degree of formality is a dimension that separates many public speaking occasions—the one-on-one briefing in the office from a briefing of a legislative subcommittee, for example. Since formal occasions tend to be more threatening than do informal occasions, part of the learning strategy is to use informal occasions as a training ground for the more formal.

### Preparation

The amount of preparation that is appropriate may be related to formality, but it is quite distinct from it. The briefing of a new project member may be quite informal and still require substantial preparation. A plan of presentation, perhaps in the form of a checklist of points to cover, and copies of materials like memos and progress reports, audiovisuals, and more might be included in preparation. The actual session may include rolled up sleeves and frequent trips to the coffee pot, but lack of good preparation can create negative results. There are many public speaking situations in which preparation is not possible or can be only partial. No speaker can prepare the answer to every possible question. Preparation is important in virtually all speaking situations. The type and degree of preparation will vary considerably from one occasion to the next.

### Interaction

The type and degree of interaction between the speaker and audience is a critical component of the public speaking scene. Sometimes, virtually no interaction is expected or called for. At other times the interaction is the core of the event. This dimension significantly affects the nature of the speaking occasion and the abilities required. The higher the interaction, the less the predictability for the speaker. On the other hand, audience feedback can be supportive and reassuring. Some persons prefer a highly interactive occasion, filled with exchange, surprise, and feedback from the audience; others like low interaction, maintaining as much predictability as possible.

### Audiovisuals and Props

For some occasions, audiovisual materials are useful and expected. For others they are used sparingly, if at all. Their use makes public speaking much more of a multisensory activity and increases the probability that the message will be conveyed and understood. Visuals and other aids can also add to the logistical complexity, cost, and preparation time. Visuals provide the opportunity for moving down on the formality scale; specifically, they reduce the need to read a speech or to be tied to notes. A well-sequenced flip chart, set of transparencies, or slides can provide all the prompts a speaker needs. The notes and word-for-word text can be eliminated. Usually this reduction in formality, along with the information conveyed by the visuals, increases the effectiveness of presentation.

## EXAMINING TYPES OF SPEAKING

Formality, preparation, interaction, and visuals are key characteristics of each of the important public speaking occasions.

### Speech

The speech provides the classic image of public speaking. The speaker delivers (even reads) a carefully prepared (sometimes word-for-word) statement with no interruptions from the audience. The occasion has a formal, almost ritualistic air to it. Audiovisuals and props are not ordinarily a part of the classic speech. It tends to be high on formality and preparation and low on interaction and visuals.

### Briefings and Presentations

The common image of a briefing (presentations and briefings are used interchangeably here) is a speaker using a pointer to focus attention on a visual display, perhaps a map, a flip chart, or a picture, diagram, or data on a screen. The audience mostly listens, but occasionally breaks in with questions and reactions. This is an event high on preparation, moderate on formality and interaction, and high on the use of visuals. Briefings may be conducted by an individual, but very frequently they involve a team.

## Meetings

A meeting participant or member of an audience is not ordinarily treated as a public speaker, but these roles are actually a form of public speaking for two reasons. For many professionals and managers it is in fact the primary occasion in which they speak before other people. Speaking done poorly here can, in the course of a year, waste hundreds of person-hours. Speaking in committee meetings, training sessions, seminars, and other situations if done well can achieve the objectives of other speaking occasions: to inform, to persuade, to entertain. The first time I recall thinking about a committee meeting as an occasion for public speaking skills was a one-hour meeting in which one person said "uh" 127 times, after I started counting. In thinking about meeting participation as a form of public speaking, do not think about it as a place to make speeches, at least not speeches as ordinarily conceived. Meeting participation is high on the interactive dimension, moderate (hopefully) on preparation, moderate to low on formality, and the use of visuals may vary.

## Interviews

An interview is also not usually treated as a public speaking occasion except in the more formal circumstance of a media interview or press conference. Again, for many, this is the occasion in which public speaking skills are most called on. It is in response to questions, often a series of questions, that many persons most frequently occupy the time of an audience. Usually the formality is low, visuals are not used, preparation is low or moderate, and interaction is high.

From a learning perspective, this broad conceptualization

of public speaking adds multiple opportunities to the list. A whole range of situations exist in which speaking skills can be practiced and put to use. Recognize, however, that these different situations require different behaviors. Adaptability is critical when moving from one to another. Yet many of the fundamental principles apply to all situations.

A simple inventory of your own public speaking patterns may indicate available learning opportunities.

During the past year, roughly how many times did you:

give a speech?

give a presentation by yourself?

give a presentation as member of a team?

attend a meeting at which you spoke?

attend a class or training session at which you asked a question or spoke about something?

were interviewed, formally or informally, by someone?

Is this profile likely to change over the next year? Five years? Fifteen? How can you use your current pattern of opportunities to become better at what you already do, or prepare for future needs?

## CHARACTERISTICS OF A QUALITY PERFORMANCE

Recognizing that public speaking is a very diverse activity, what are the characteristics of good performance? Are they different from one type of speaking occasion to the next? The greater the commonality, the more there is an opportunity to develop skill in one circumstance and transfer it to another.

### Fits Audience

Experts on public speaking may disagree about a number of things, but there is clear consensus that an effective performance is one geared to the characteristics of the audience. That does not mean telling the audience only what it wants to hear. Sometimes the message, by necessity, may be bad news. Politicians sometimes get into trouble by wanting to tell a specific audience just what it wants to hear, and then to follow the principle, have to give a different story to another audience that wants to hear something else. So meeting audience needs does not mean sacrificing truth or integrity.

Audience fit requires answering questions like these: How much does the audience know about the subject? How much background information is needed to make sure an audience is able to understand the key points? How does the audience feel about the topic? Does the audience have any preconceived notions about you? How much detail will the audience want or expect? How large is the audience (primarily of concern for handouts, visuals, and forms interaction might take)?

Adapting a public speaking performance to these questions is appropriate no matter which of the forms the performance takes—whether a speech, a briefing, a meeting, or in response to an interview. If there is a high level of interaction, adjustments can be made during the course of the performance if the speaker is appropriately prepared. The lower level of interaction in most speeches makes timely adaptation difficult, but not impossible. Yawns or irritation or enjoyment may be picked up even in a speech situation.

### Fits Occasion

Closely related to matching the audience is matching the occasion. Is it a celebration or a somber occasion? Is the presentation an input into a decision? Is the performance expected to influence behavior of the audience?

## Serves Intended Purpose

The traditional view is that public speaking can be divided into three purposes: to inform, to persuade, and to entertain. Stretching these terms only slightly, if at all, the case can be made that all public speaking occasions should meet all three purposes, just to different degrees. These purposes can be thought of as mutually reinforcing. Information is often the best persuader (Jackson 1988), and entertainment can enhance receptiveness to information. Similarly, all four of the public speaking types, speeches, briefings, meetings, and interviews, should or at least can contain all three purposes. Speeches should inform, entertain, and persuade (even if only to persuade the audience that the topic is important). Of course the portion of each will vary considerably, and one is likely to be dominant. An effective presentation has the right proportions of each.

A presentation or briefing should also have elements of informing, persuading, and entertaining. These almost always are geared for a high proportion of informing. Persuading can be high on the purpose list too, but that varies. Sometimes persuading, at least to a particular point of view about what should be done, is a minimal objective; sometimes it is the primary purpose. Entertainment, in the form of humor or simply engagement in the "story" that is being unfolded, is not often the ultimate purpose, but it is a minor one that can help achieve the others.

The intent of a participant in a meeting, as opposed to the purpose of the meeting itself, may also be all three. An effective performance by someone in a meeting clearly may require informing others, or persuading others, or both. Entertainment is a feature too. Dull meeting talk may cause participants to ignore what the speaker is saying, and the opportunity to inform and persuade is lost. Humor clearly has a place in breaking tension and sometimes in breaking monotony. The critical point in thinking about one's role in a meeting as entertainment is proportion. One well-timed bit of humor is probably effective, the second is okay, but the third may well be overkill.

Thinking of the effectiveness of one's performance in responding to an interview also calls on all three purposes. Clearly, in some circumstances, entertainment can be the primary purpose of one's role. Guests on Johnny Carson's "The Tonight Show" are well aware of this. Keep it in mind if you are being interviewed by the written press as well. Furthermore, it may be an effective although not major ingredient in almost every other interview situation. Still, informing and persuading are the principal tasks of the public speaker as interviewee.

The principal point, then, is that informing, persuading, and entertaining may be appropriate purposes of all public speaking occasions. The relative proportions, though, are likely to be quite different. The degree of effectiveness goes way up when the proportions are right, and it goes down dramatically when the proportions are skewed.

### Engages Audience

An effective public speaking performance is one that engages the audience (Meuse 1988: 132). An engaged audience is attentive, responsive, involved, and sometimes but not always supportive. Some of the characteristics of speaker performance that help an audience become engaged are commitment to the subject, energy, clarity of argument, and interaction. Again, these apply to all four speaking types, although in differing ways.

*Commitment to subject.* If a speaker does not believe what he or she is saying, it is quite likely the audience will not believe it either. The converse is also true. "If a speaker knows what he wants to say, *really* wants to say it, and wants everybody in that room to understand what the hell it is he wants to say, all the other things, like looking people in the eye and using good gestures, will just come naturally (R. T. Kingman as quoted in Leech 1982: 11)." In most cases, it is not belief or its absence, but level of interest shown by the speaker that determines whether the audience will or is able to become engaged. The most global advice to you as a speaker might be to organize your life and work so you spend your time on the things that really interest you.

Although only working with matters about which we have a passionate commitment or even strong interest may be good advice, it is not always achievable. We find ourselves meeting about subjects, being interviewed about matters, giving briefings on projects, and even giving speeches about subjects that are two or three rungs down on our priority list. If possible and reasonable, turn down second- and third-level interest speaking opportunities, whether they are speeches or committee assignments. However, since that is not always possible and every topic is not of the greatest interest, it may be necessary to fake it, to invest as much enthusiasm as possible into the matter we are stuck with. Sometimes generating enthusiasm is necessary even on topics of great interest. On days when you feel a cold coming on, when you are tired from an earlier deadline, and when the transmission just went out on your car, commitment to a subject may not come naturally. Finding a way to focus your attention and show interest and enthusiasm for the topic is important for speaking effectiveness.

*Energy.* A high energy level is a close companion to commitment to subject. If you have a strong interest in a topic, it is much easier to show a high energy level. If you show a high energy level, it will appear that you have a strong interest in the topic. And, this can provide a real payoff, because if you show a high energy level your interest in the topic is likely to go up—at least for that speaking occasion. So, if you can force or psych yourself up to a high energy level to begin a speaking session, the chances are you will become genuinely involved yourself, and a natural momentum will carry you on through.

A problem for speakers, one that occurs most frequently on the more formal speaking occasions, is the inability to let the natural interest in a topic show through in a high-energy way. Nervousness, or the formality of the situation, imposes an energy reducer. The adrenalin of stage fright is held in check to the point that a very low energy level is expressed. An effective performance lets that energy show through.

*Clarity and quality of content.* It is not simply performance in a speaking situation that engages an audience. Equally, perhaps more, important, is the clarity and quality of the content conveyed. Whether in a speech, briefing, meeting, or interview, if you have nothing worthwhile to say, the audience will not be captivated. Let's assume that quality content is taken care of and focus on a few points about clarity.

An engaging speaking performance, whether for a minute or an hour, typically has several recognizable characteristics. One is to assure the stage is set or the context established. In a high-interactive situation, this may already be established and require little of the speaker's attention. In others, it may be the most important aspect of engaging the audience. Setting the stage may mean letting the audience know the central theme of a speech, or clearly stating the objective a presentation is intended to achieve, or restating a problem a motion is intended to address, or providing background information in relation to a question.

A second feature of clarity that is engaging is to establish a sequence or a logic you intend to follow and then let the audience in on the sequence. An audience usually appreciates knowing where the speaker is headed and where he or she is at any time in the process. It also helps the speaker.

Appropriate level of detail is another feature of an engaging presentation. This is closely linked to the type of audience and the type of occasion. A briefing to instruct a group of personnel officers how to implement a new policy clearly requires more detail than a briefing on the same policy to a group of executive directors who only need to know the broad outlines. Clarity can be obscured by too much or too little information. Error in level of detail is quite common and can easily disengage an audience.

Visuals accompanying an oral presentation can add immeasurably to clarity and do a great deal to get an audience intellectually and emotionally involved. Opportunities to add clarity to an argument are often missed because of poor or no visuals at all. Visuals range from extraordinarily simple to quite sophisticated. Sometimes the simple ones are not used enough. It is relatively rare, for example, for a participant in a meeting to go to the easel pad or blackboard and sketch the main points in a proposal. A simple visual by a speechmaker with the main points visible to the audience throughout can be helpful. Pictures can sometimes engage an audience in important ways. Numbers, if important enough to be included, are usually made more effective if they are visually displayed. Visuals that don't do the job can turn the interest level of an audience down in a hurry. Avoid visuals with too much information and those that cannot be seen by anyone sitting past the front row.

*Interaction.* If effective interaction is occurring, it is highly likely that the audience is engaged with the speaker. There are several factors to look for in interaction between speaker and audience. One of the most important, and often ignored, is eye contact (Meuse 1988: 155). Almost every book about speaking and presentations emphasizes its role in an effective presentation. Most speakers, after developing eye contact skill, consider it a very satisfying part of a presentation. Short cuts to eye contact are generally not effective. For example, looking at a spot on the wall behind the audience just might cause a person in the audience to turn around to see what is wrong with the wall. It definitely is no substitute for real visual connection with listeners. In a modest-sized audience, and certainly in an audience of one or two, there should be definite eye contact with everyone. Such contact is interaction because it is two-way communication; the speaker as well as the audience is receiving information. This is one of those habits that is easy to work on in daily, low-threat situations. Every conversation is an opportunity to cultivate the eye-contact habit.

Interaction is often enhanced when a speaker escapes from behind the lectern or the speakers' table. It is a clear gesture toward making audience contact when the speaker moves from such protective barriers and even more so if he or she leaves the written text behind as well. The very behavior of the speaker is likely to be changed, usually for the better. Moving from behind protective barriers applies to non-speech situations too. The requirement of managing visuals often brings a presenter from behind protective furniture. An interviewee may need to make an effort to avoid a desk getting in the way.

Encouraging questions from an audience is a step toward interaction. Some speakers are very poised and skilled at handling questions and really come alive in the question-and-answer session. Others, if they could, would skip it entirely. It is a desirable skill to have (Meuse 1988: 169). On the right occasion, a question-and-answer session can have greater impact than the presentation that stimulated it. Besides, it is not always possible to dictate whether there will or will not be one. It is better to have the skill ready at hand.

Carrying questions and answers another step toward interaction is to involve the audience in discussion. Just like question and answer, this is not always possible or appropriate. The formality of the situation may preclude it. At a presidential state of the union address, question and answer would seem out of place; at a presidential news conference, a discussion, as much as some of the press might like it, would be inappropriate. There are many circumstances though, in which a fully interactive discussion with the audience is highly desirable. Many ideal opportunities for such interaction are missed. It is a step a speaker can encourage and manage.

### Timing and Closing

When and how to stop is as important as any other aspect of public speaking in all four variations. Speakers' joke books have an ample supply of quips, one-liners, and stories about the negative consequences of speakers going on too long, yet it continues to be a problem. Fear of stopping can be as strong as the fear of public speaking itself. A speaker who announces up front that he or she will be brief may be especially dangerous. During one stretch I kept score on speakers who made just that promise. Seven in a row spoke beyond the announced time period; three of them more than doubled the planned speaking time. Maybe speakers who say they will be brief do so because they are not well prepared and fear that they have very little to say. Since their remarks are not well organized, it takes them a long time to say a little. And of course, the sound of one's own voice is mesmerizing. A speaker, presenter, meeting participant, and interviewee are all well advised to say less than they might like. An audience seldom is upset because a speech ended a few minutes early.

How to end is important, especially for speeches and presentations. And, of course, the ending is especially important for a sales presentation (Peoples 1988) since the ending is directly related to the purpose—making a sale. The character of an effective ending of any presentation, including a highly interactive one, is dependent on purpose.

If informing is the primary objective, especially if a large amount of information has been delivered, a summary of main points may be the most effective way to conclude. If action is the desired result, the finale may best focus on just what decision or behavior is expected or agreed upon. The error to avoid in all situations is just to stop, although that is better than just to keep going. The success of a public speaking occasion often is dependent on what happens after it is over, so an effective speaker takes advantage of the closing to shape what happens.

## STEPS TO A QUALITY PERFORMANCE

The several pages above offer a sketch of effective performance in a variety of public speaking situations. This section develops a few suggestions we can use to perform more consistently at a high level in the public-speaking arena. The development of any skill builds on itself. The more skillful, the greater the confidence; the greater the confidence, the easier it is to build the next level of skill. The progression may be especially true of public speaking. The same progression may carry over from one skill to the next (Gard 1986).

### Positive Anticipation

The long-range goal every professional and manager should set in the area of public speaking is to achieve a level of skill and confidence so that any opportunity for public speaking is something looked forward to with positive anticipation. A request to make a presentation, if this goal is achieved, becomes a treat. For some people that attitude is probably hard to imagine. It is possible to achieve, though. I have seen more than one person move from having shaky knees and cracking voice to having a true enjoyment of the process. When that attitude of enjoyment, of positive anticipation, is achieved, the odds of effective public speaking go up whether making a speech, doing a briefing, or participating in a meeting or interview. That attitude does not mean that you will never feel nervous or have some jitters, but it is likely to remove the really inhibiting fear that can get in the way of an effective public performance.

Someone once drew an analogy between public speaking and walking on a foot-wide board ten feet long. For most, walking such a board if it were one foot off the ground could be done with little effort. We would be quite relaxed and probably bet that we could walk it a hundred times without falling. Now raise the board 100 feet in the air. Our attitude is likely to change dramatically. Most of us would probably refuse to walk it. If we did accept, or were forced or pressured into walking it, our attitude would be quite different than it was at the one-foot height. Now instead of being relaxed, we would be nervous and tense, and our ability to walk the board successfully would probably be greatly reduced. Yet the task is the same. It is primarily attitude that is different.

Our inhibitions about public speaking are very much like the fear of walking a board 100 feet off the ground. Walking the board at one foot is easy, like talking to one person. Walking at 100 feet is frightening, perhaps like talking to 100 people. The trick to walking the board is to lower it— mentally if not physically. Don't look down. The trick for a 100 people, or a million, is to find an equivalent of lowering the board. Perhaps the board should be placed at five feet— high enough to keep us alert, but not bring out the debilitating inhibitions.

Taking out the inhibitions and replacing them with free-flowing energy is the key transition. It is the same transition required in moving from a tense, halting writer to an energetic and quick one. That can occur by a series of successes, beginning with low-threat occasions. Build successes and move on. If a failure happens, learn from it; focus on what it would take to make it successful and lasting. Viewing public speaking in broad terms, take advantage of the many opportunities for practicing in low-threat situations. Use the natural practice opportunities that are available.

## SELF-DIRECTED IMPROVEMENT STRATEGIES

Many resources are readily accessible for improving speaking skill, including regular learning and practice opportunities at work and leisure. Finding the right strategy and then getting started are the important steps. The resources and ideas that follow are intended to offer a broad menu, more than you might want to pursue. The central idea is for you to develop your own approach, one that fits your personality, your profession, your work environment, and the time you can devote to it. Then stick to it. The absence of time, however, is not an acceptable reason for doing nothing. Begin with an approach that takes a minimal amount of time, one that can be intertwined with your normal responsibilities.

### Books

Reading what other people have to say about speaking is one useful approach. Many speakers and presenters have written about their experiences and about their observations of others in action. Much of the literature is experience-based and hence has a very pragmatic "how to" style. A small sample of available books follows, but a trip to a library or the "self-help" section of a bookstore, or attention to ads in professional journals or mailed announcements, will produce many worthy additions.

Alexander, Roy. (1986). *Power Speech*. New York: AMACOM.
Alexander makes the argument that speaking, from speech-making to conversation, is critical to career success. The book focuses on the proper enunciation and pronunciation

of words—power words—that will either make or break your speech. It discusses how to choose, create, and update your choice of words, suggests ways to improve your voice, to be persuasive, to motivate, to use humor, and other topics.

Bower, Sharon A. (1981). *Painless Public Speaking.* Englewood Cliffs, N.J.: Prentice-Hall, Inc. This handbook discusses ways to desensitize yourself to anxiety and to develop self-confidence by using the "train of thought" method.

Coulter, Carol, Ann Duke, Machelle Curtis, and Kim Mitterling. (1982). *Winning Words: A New Approach to Developing Effective Speaking Skills.* Boston: CBI Publishing Company. An entertaining book built around a series of hypothetical conversations between an authority and an aspiring speaker. It provides series of checklists, assessment inventories, and other worksheets. An accompanying audio cassette is available.

DiGaetani, John Louis, ed. (1986). *The Handbook of Executive Communication.* Homewood, Ill.: Dow Jones-Irwin. Contains a section with several separately authored chapters on speaking along with other sections on writing and interviewing. A very comprehensive guide to communication in an organizational setting.

Doolittle, Robert J. (1984). *Professionally Speaking: A Concise Guide.* Glenview, Ill.: Scott, Foresman. The emphasis in this book is on a thinking and planning process that precedes the preparation of public speeches.

Dunckel, Jacqueline, and Elizabeth Parnham. (1985). *The Business Guide to Effective Speaking.* London: Kogan Page. A short (122 pages) but wide-ranging book covering a variety of topics about speaking. It is unique in presenting almost all of the text in bullet form.

Flacks, Niki, and Robert W. Rasberry. (1982). *Power Talk: How to Use Theater Techniques to Win Your Audience.* New York: The Free Press. Written by a professional actress and an organizational communications specialist, this book focuses on the application of acting techniques to public presentations.

Gard, Grant G. (1986). *The Art of Confident Public Speaking.* Englewood Cliffs, N.J.: Prentice-Hall. A practical guide to speechmaking.

Holcombe, Marya W., and Judith K. Stein. (1983). *Presentations for Decision Makers: Strategies for Structuring and Delivering Your Ideas.* Belmont, Calif.: Lifetime Learning Publications. Offers a process for developing a presentation or briefing similar to their book on writing. Using an organization tree to order thinking and determine priorities is a feature.

Leech, Thomas. (1982). *How To Prepare, Stage, and Deliver Winning Presentations.* New York: AMACOM. Presents a comprehensive approach to presentations, including a strong statement about the importance of presentations for corporate and career success.

Meuse, Leonard F., Jr. (1988). *Succeeding at Business and Technical Presentations.* 2d ed. New York: John Wiley & Sons. With a focus on presentations and briefings rather than speeches, this book includes extensive guidelines for producing and using visuals with a variety of technology.

Simmons, S. H. (1982). *How to Be the Life of the Podium.* New York: AMACOM. A collection of anecdotes and stories from a professional speechwriter interspersed with advice about the process of constructing a speech.

## Journals and Magazines

Like writing, various popular magazines and professional journals occasionally carry articles with tips on speaking effectively. *The Toastmaster* is a monthly magazine, published by Toastmasters International, devoted exclusively to public speaking.

## Tapes and Videos

Audio and video tapes are a resource especially well adapted to the topic of speaking. A variety of both audio and video tapes is available; each has its advantages. The real advantage of audio cassette tapes is the ability to fit them into dead time, for instance, when driving. Commuters, alone or with carpoolers of similar interests, can acquire a vast amount of information in a year's time whether about speaking or a myriad of other professionally relevant topics. Both "how to" tapes and samples of speeches are available. Many famous speeches, some of them recordings of actual speeches and others reenactments, are available.

Video tapes usually require dedicated time, but have the obvious advantage of the full visual setting. Both "how to" and actual presentations and speeches are available. Toastmasters, for example, produced *Be Prepared to Speak: The Step-by-Step Video Guide to Public Speaking.* It dramatizes a reluctant speaker going through the decision to accept an invitation to the actual (highly successful, of course) presentation.

## Classes/Workshops

The opportunity for formal training in public speaking is readily available in most locations. Government, business, and nonprofit organizations sponsor training programs in speaking on a recurring basis. Some focus on delivering speeches and some on presentations. Free-standing fee-based workshops are regular occurrences. Community colleges, colleges, and universities usually have courses in public speaking, and professional and technical presentation skills in some cases, as well as theater and other communication subjects.

## Toastmasters

Toastmasters International offers ready-made opportunities for developing speaking skills. It comprises a network of local clubs throughout the United States and a number of other countries. A city of any size is likely to have a number of clubs, some free standing and some associated with a business or government organization. A variety of meeting times, places, and frequencies is often available. Some meet weekly and some every two weeks. Some meet at lunch, some at the dinner hour, and some without a meal involved.

From my experience with several chapters, the club supports the development of speaking skill in a supportive, nonthreatening environment. They provide an opportunity to progress from novice to accomplished professional through a series of speech types along with the chance to give occasional impromptu speeches. Both receiving and giving feedback is an integral part of the program. For the adventuresome, speaking contests are organized with the opportunity in some of them to progress to the international level.

## Critically Listening to Others

Most professionals and managers listen to a multitude of speeches, presentations, meeting discussions, and interview responses. This may be the best learning opportunity available. Listen and watch with an eye toward shaping your own skills. What works? What does not? What works for someone else, but may not suit your personality or style? What are mistakes others make that you can avoid? If you are the systematic type, keep a running file of ideas to try, use, and avoid.

This kind of critical observation can be done in the normal course of your work and leisure activities, but it may be worth taking in some additional events. Seek out the presenter or speaker who is known to be especially effective and watch him or her in action. Also, take in the not-so-well regarded. It is sometimes especially revealing to observe someone who does the same thing you do. As a college professor, for example, I find it very informative to audit or, to get the full effect, take a class taught by someone else. The pitfalls and the virtues stand out.

Critically observing from a self-learning perspective is not simply a matter of evaluating how well another speaker performs, although that is part of it. The purpose is to identify the factors that make a difference so you can capture them for your own use. Here are some questions to keep in mind:

• Does the speaker engage the audience? If so, how?

• What does the speaker do to set the stage, to let the audience in on context and purpose? Is it a technique I can use?

• Is there a technique for using visuals that I can adopt?

• Does the speaker use concrete examples in an especially effective way? Can I follow the example in my own professional area?

• What can I learn from how the speaker handles hostile questions?

• Are there any annoyances I can avoid?

• Is there an identifiable reason the speaker is obscure about some points?

Answers to questions like these add up to an important body of information about how to and how not to make speeches, presentations, participate in meetings, and respond to interviews. If used, it is probably better than reading a dozen books on the topic.

## Creating and Using Practice Opportunities

Volumes of critical observation of others would do little to improve your own skill development without actually doing it yourself. It would be no better than reading by itself. The critical step, then, is to use the opportunities for speaking that already exist and create new opportunities that carry you beyond your current level.

Using current opportunities simply involves continuing to do what you are doing, but with the addition of using them as occasions for improvement. What has been learned from reading or from critical observation or your own thinking about what would make for a better performance can be brought into play. New ideas can be tried and old habits discarded.

Creating new opportunities can be done in many ways depending on your environment. At one level it might simply mean speaking up when before you would have remained silent. At a meeting of a professional society, make the effort to ask the speaker a question or participate in the discussion. Creating new opportunities may also mean things like joining the company speakers' bureau or volunteering to speak to a class or some of the many other means to get yourself before an audience. It might even mean an audience of one. Volunteer to tutor a student in your specialty area or teach a new employee the database program your organization uses.

### Feedback

Feedback is important for skill development in speaking as well as writing. And also like writing, getting feedback can profitably occur at several stages in the process. It does not just mean having someone evaluate a formal presentation or speech, although that is certainly appropriate and useful. Feedback may also mean trying out ideas in advance of a presentation.

Making the effort to provide feedback to others is also useful for honing your own ideas about speaking. If you can work with one or more people in a mutually supportive way, feedback can be handled in a routine and, ideally, non-threatening way. This is a major reason a club environment can be so helpful.

### Self-Feedback

Assessing your own performance is an important form of feedback. Don't neglect it, but neither be too soft nor too hard on yourself. Use it to design a more effective performance the next time, not as criticism for a poor performance. An important part of self-feedback is awareness of how performance in currently nonthreatening occasions can be transferred to more-threatening ones. Reinforce the skills required to brief a work team, and recognize them as the same skills required to make a presentation to a committee of the state legislature.

Put technology to work by taping one or more of your nonthreatening speaking occasions, or a practice session, then grit your teeth and play it back. Audio taping is quite informative, but at least once or twice make a videotape.

### Experiment/Push Yourself

If you are already relatively accomplished as a speaker, think about moving to the next plateau. If you are a regular at company presentations, take the step as a lunchtime speaker at a local service club. If you have traditionally stood behind the lectern and relied heavily on notes, make a presentation in front of the lectern. Instead of simply responding to questions in some session, turn it into a short open discussion. Try new ideas. Don't get trapped at one level or in one mode, even if it is a good one.

### STRATEGY FOR THE FEARFUL

What if you have a real apprehension about speaking? You have consistently avoided all occasions that require anything remotely resembling speaking in public. It is an apprehension you want to overcome, but so far you have been unable. (For the extreme case of someone with a true phobia, professional consultation may be required.) The principal idea is one that has been mentioned throughout this chapter—start with some activity that is now relatively comfortable, treat it as a beginning public speaking occasion, develop confidence, and gradually progress to the next level or the next type of activity. These first steps may be very simple. For me some years ago as a student it was asking questions in class. Part of the preparation I began to make, after three years of speaking in class only when called on, was to develop a question or two beforehand. If the situation allowed and my courage was adequate that day, I would ask a question. Soon I didn't need to prepare a question before class but began to ask more spontaneously. To this day I enjoy asking a question or two after a speech or presentation.

The specific technique of formulating questions in advance may not be your choice for becoming comfortable at the sound of your voice in front of an audience. But there probably is an equivalent.

## MOTIVATION TO START AND CONTINUE

It is easy to put off working on public speaking as a skill. There may be a tendency to hope the need does not arise and when it does to get by and be glad when it is over. The point is that most of us are already, somewhat unknowingly, involved in public speaking far more than we think. One strategy for improvement is to make the most of what we are already doing and build on it.

For those who have apprehension, which is probably most of us, advice to "just relax, there is no reason to be concerned" is clearly inadequate and even false. There are too many stories of promotions not received because of bombing out in the briefing room. In fact, the stakes can be high, although usually it is not one blown presentation but many mediocre ones over a period of time that create the problem. In either case, beginning a steady program of improvement solidly based in what you already do can provide the skill necessary for the many little speaking occasions as well as the few big ones.

## REFERENCES

Gard, Grant G. (1986). *The Art of Confident Public Speaking.* Englewood Cliffs, N.J.: Prentice-Hall.

Jackson, Dale E. (1988). *Interpersonal Communication for Technically Trained Managers: A Guide to Skills and Techniques.* New York: Quorum Books.

Leech, Thomas. (1982). *How to Prepare, Stage, and Deliver Winning Presentations.* New York: AMACOM.

Meuse, Leonard F., Jr. (1988). *Succeeding at Business and Technical Presentations.* 2d ed. New York: John Wiley & Sons.

Peoples, David A. (1988). *Presentations Plus.* New York: John Wiley & Sons.

# 4

---

# Interviewing: A Skill for All Professionals

## THE FREQUENCY AND VARIETY OF INTERVIEWING

Some years back, I was trekking in the hills of Nepal. Actually, I was there on a two-year Peace Corps assignment, and walking was the only way to get from one place to another in the mountains. So trekking is a romantic term for what at times was simply a chore. The local Nepalese took the human trait of wanting to provide good news to an extreme, so any question about distance to the next town always resulted in the same answer, some variation of "not very far." When I wanted accurate information about distance, good interviewing skill was necessary. Treks became occasions to practice interviewing.

Interviewing is sometimes thought of as a specialized activity done for things like hiring, opinion polling, news reporting, and conversing with celebrities on talk shows. Certainly those are good examples of interviewing, but similar interviewing skills are desirable in many other situations. They can be used every day in both professional and personal activities. You do not need to be in Barbara Walters' profession for interviewing skill to be valuable. In fact, there is hardly a profession that could not benefit from skill as an interviewer. Here is a partial listing of professionals who need interviewing skill.

architects

engineers

clergy

family counselors

salespersons

teachers

administrators

guidance counselors

systems analysts

social workers

reporters

nurses

physicians

dentists

lawyers

organization analysts

social scientists

police

personnel managers

psychiatrists and psychologists

The quality of a product or service and the satisfaction of a patient, client, customer, or student often depend on the quality of the interview that accompanies the product or service.

Interviewing is a process that is used in all types of organizations, public, private, and nonprofit. We interview for employee performance. We interview prospective employees as well as those leaving. An attorney interviews clients in order to obtain the facts in a case. A physician interviews a patient to help diagnose an illness. An accountant interviews a client about income tax deductions.

Like writing and public speaking, interviewing skill can be useful in our personal lives as well. We interview our children, mechanics, clothing salespersons, and even fellow travelers we pass on the trail. Often, interviewing is an unconscious action, but we all do it whether we call it interviewing or not.

Despite its regularity, interviewing, formally and informally, is often not done well. Some personnel specialists think that typical employment interviews do almost nothing to improve and indeed even sometimes reduce the chances of selecting effective employees. Physicians, teachers, and others often exhibit poor interviewing skills, despite its importance (Dillon 1990). Most of us can recall incidents in which we did not get the information we needed or did not achieve the results we wanted because of poor questioning and interview technique.

## What Is It?

Many definitions can be found in the literature and practice of interviewing. One definition appealing for its simplicity is found in Mabery's (1980: 10) book for young adults on interviewing celebrities: "An interview is a meeting in which one person obtains information from another person." A discussion of interviewing in *The Handbook of Executive Communication* (Henze 1986: 635) emphasizes three features of interviewing: (1) a conversation, (2) with a purpose, and (3) a time limit. For others, a key feature is questioning, one person asking another person one or a series of questions (Dillon 1990). Let us settle on a definition of interviewing as a purposeful exchange of information between two or more persons in which questioning is an important feature.

This view of interviewing is purposefully broad; it encourages professionals and managers to treat more conversations and meetings as interviews. This treatment can improve the effectiveness and efficiency of many such exchanges (Henze 1986) as well as provide a broader training ground for the development of more-effective interviewing skill.

Treating various exchanges as interviews can make them better. First, it can make an interaction more purposeful. A lunch, for example, can be a focus for real information exchange rather a small-talk affair. It may turn out to be more enjoyable and interesting as well. Second, the interview orientation, whether in an informal or formal exchange, can focus attention on the quality of questions and the overall exchange. Such attention can sharpen and improve the interaction. Third, if you think of an interview as an interaction with a time limit, boundaries can be placed on exchanges that otherwise might continue on after their purpose has been served. Finally, if done well and without prying, the interview orientation may demonstrate an interest in the other person that might not otherwise be perceived. As Dale Carnegie showed, expressing an interest in the other person and what he or she does is powerful and appreciated.

Building on the idea of learning from what you already do, almost any conversation can become an opportunity to improve interviewing ability and habits. Since so many ordinary exchanges are interviews, interviewing practice should become a habit. At first it may be necessary consciously to label an upcoming conversation as an interview and switch to "interview mode," but ideally the conscious switch will become unnecessary. These opportunities allow practice and self-reflection. Did I ask the right question in the right way and really hear the response?

## Purposes and Types of Interviewing

The multiple purposes of interviewing sometimes create confusion. One view is that interviewing is done simply for the purpose of obtaining information. That clearly is a major purpose for interviewing, but not the only one. Changing the behavior of one or both participants in an interview is also an important purpose. These two purposes, obtaining information and changing behavior, can be thought of as a continuum along which various types of interviews fall.

obtain information ------------------------------------ change behavior

The objective of some interviews, a research interview for example, is to gain information in as pure a form as possible with no influence on the interviewee. Researchers worry that the fact of the interview itself may inject some change in the attitude and behavior of the interviewee and therefore contaminate the results. A sales interview is at the other end of the spectrum. The very purpose of the interview is to change attitude and behavior—to encourage the prospect to reach the conclusion that product x is needed. Getting the sale may involve acquiring a large amount of information, but it is not the information alone that is of value. Similarly, an interview between a physician and a patient requires information exchange, but it includes more. The patient must end up with the conviction that it is important to take the medicine prescribed. Most interviews are in fact a mixture of obtaining information and changing behavior; most fall somewhere in the middle of the continuum. That is one reason they are a dynamic, interesting, and powerful form of interaction. Consider some of the types of interviews common enough to have labels.

selection interview

exit interview

performance appraisal interview

counseling interview

information interview

negotiation interview

sales interview

disciplinary interview

opinion poll

career-planning interview

diagnostic interview

news interview

broadcast interview

Many of these interview occasions are one-to-one, but some lend themselves well to a group interview. The "group" may be on either side of the interview. Many job candidates are interviewed by a selection panel, for example. A variety of circumstances may dictate interviewing a number of respondents simultaneously.

## CHARACTERISTICS OF EFFECTIVE INTERVIEWING

Specialized interviews abound. However, since most professionals and managers conduct many types of interviews, it is worth focusing on features that apply to many or all specialized types. Among other things, this keeps specialized interviewing in perspective. There is specific literature and guidance about most specialty interviews. A larger framework can be helpful to place that in context.

### Roles

The normal conception of an interview is that one person is in charge, that one person asks the questions and the other answers. In many cases this is exactly the relationship. If we are called on the telephone by the Gallup organization and asked our opinions about presidential candidates and current public-policy problems, we assume we will be answering, not asking questions. If we are willing to cooperate, we relinquish most of the control to the pollster. Despite their awkwardness, *interviewer* and *interviewee* have become commonly used words.

In other circumstances, it is primarily hierarchy that determines who is considered the interviewer and who the interviewee. An employment interview ordinarily places the employer in the dominant role associated with the interviewer and the applicant in the more subordinate interviewee role. Similarly, a doctor and patient, a police officer and suspect, and others follow the question-asker–question-answerer pattern.

Many interviews do not follow the classic pattern, however. An interview may be an exchange in which neither controls the agenda. A good interview could have an equal number of questions asked and answered by each party. Employment interviews can take on this two-way relationship. Usually, the higher the level of the prospective employee, the more the interview becomes a two-way exchange. An entry-level employee will ordinarily accede to the agenda-setting power of the employer. A candidate for a top-level executive position is not as likely to do so. Indeed, the relationship may even tip, with the candidate setting the agenda. This occurs with some regularity in news interviews in which a reporter is interviewing a high-level politician or diplomat. Each may be struggling to shape the agenda, to address the issues each wants to cover and to avoid others. In some cases the interview becomes a contest of power and will.

Both parties in the interview may be involved in shaping the agenda and in giving and receiving information. The checklist for effective interviewing needs to be considered appropriate for both parties.

### Key Features

A simple checklist provides a framework for planning, participating in, and evaluating an interview.

1. Did the interview take place in the right atmosphere? *Atmosphere* encompasses several factors, including time, place, and conditions.
2. Were the right questions asked? This focuses on the substantive agenda of the interview. It refers to topics covered as well as the form of questions. It assumes that questions may come from all parties in the interview.
3. Was there an adequate and appropriate response? This refers to the scope, depth, and focus of information exchanged.
4. Were both questions and responses fully heard? Understanding must be good in both directions; any necessary information recorded.

These simple questions may give the impression that an interview is a routine exchange that follows the same pattern each time. Not so. There is flexibility. Because of the many purposes interviews serve, that flexibility is essential.

The checklist is appropriate for both parties in the exchange. Although the degree of control may be different from one situation to the next, the interviewee should also be concerned about the effectiveness of the interview. He or she may have substantial opportunity to shape the interview, before, during, and after.

*Did the interview take place in the right atmosphere?* An effective interview can take place anywhere: on a beach in the Caribbean, in an executive suite, or over the phone. A hallway conversation, an exchange in a meeting, or talk over drinks could have the features of an effective interview, but they could also be wrong and inappropriate. It depends on the character of the interview, the relationship of the persons involved, and the atmosphere surrounding them.

The first question about atmosphere may be whether an interview is desirable at all. Perhaps for the purpose at hand, a memo or a questionnaire would do a better or more-efficient job. Moving to a questionnaire clearly changes the atmosphere, although it does serve some of the same functions as an interview.

Most formal interviews are best held somewhere free from distractions and interruptions. Sometimes this can be effectively accomplished by a closed door and instructions to hold calls. In some environments, the press of activity does not allow uninterrupted time. In situations in which you are the one taking the initiative for an interview, but protocol or courtesy requires that you go to the other person, it can be difficult to create a block of uninterrupted time. Sometimes the best solution is a neutral site outside the other person's office: a conference room, a restaurant, a hotel lobby, or a variety of other places.

Sometimes the best physical environment cannot be created. The flexibility to make the best of a less-than-ideal situation becomes a virtue. I have interviewed in a group office, in homes with the phone ringing and children crying, and in automobiles. Not ideal, but workable.

Other aspects of the interview context or atmosphere are important. One of the most critical is the manner in which an interview is arranged. A key feature in every single case is respect for the time and schedule of the other person. Mutual convenience is the ideal, but if that is not possible, the general rule should be that the person initiating an interview defer to the convenience of the other. Of course, there may be exceptions. The reason is not simply respect for the other person, although that would be adequate, but the desire to create the conditions under which the interviewee is cooperative and responsive.

Some interviews are appropriately ad hoc in character. They are initiated on the spot without prior arrangement. This is appropriate for some interviews and quite ineffective for others. If privacy, the need for materials and preparation, or other factors don't prevent it, useful interviews can be conducted on the run or in what would otherwise be wasted time, such as lunch, while driving, or walking to a meeting. There are important caveats with impromptu interviews, though; make sure that an inadequate interview is not being substituted for an adequate one. A quick hallway conversation might be considered by the other party to be adequate and make him or her unwilling to see the need for another meeting. A second caveat is that an interview on the fly may not capture the full attention of the other person and may result in inadequate information or an unconsidered response. It could result in a "no" when a more focused interview could have produced a "yes."

The general principle regarding atmosphere is to create the conditions in which the interview can succeed. That usually means creating the time and space in which two people can focus attention on the matter at hand. It also means an environment in which there are no inhibitors to an open and honest exchange of information. Doing what you can to assure the other person is in a cooperative mood is part of the task.

*Were the right questions asked?* Questions are the key ingredient in interviews. They are arrived at by many routes. In a telephone opinion poll, questions have been carefully crafted, have probably gone through a dozen drafts, and been pretested more than once. Other questions are formulated on the spur of the moment in the middle of a conversation. Both routes to questions are appropriate in their place.

A structure of four types of interviews with corresponding questions is useful for thinking through which kinds of questions are appropriate under which conditions (Patton 1980: 206).

1. Informal Conversational Interview. This type of interview is close to an ordinary conversation, but is nonetheless purposeful. Questions in an interview of this kind come out of their immediate context. While a purpose or theme for the interview is determined in advance, the specific questions are not predetermined. The specific points to be covered, the wording of questions, and the sequence are all decisions made during the interview itself.

2. Interview Guide. Using an interview guide, the topics to be covered are determined in advance, but the exact wording and sequence are left undefined until the interview. Question order and phrasing can be altered depending on the flow of the interview. In fact, all questions may not need to be asked as such. If a topic comes up in the discussion and is adequately covered, no question is required. From the interviewee's perspective, it may be difficult to tell the difference between an interview guide approach and an informal conversational interview.

3. Standardized Open-Ended Interview. All questions and the order of questions are decided in advance. The questions are open-ended in the sense that the respondent can answer in his or her own words. Every person interviewed is asked the same questions in the same order, making all interviews comparable. This format does not permit tailoring questions to the individual. Legal concerns in hiring have pushed many employment interviews to or toward this form. It is also particularly appropriate when the desired outcome is a summary of many people's responses.

4. Closed Quantitative Interview. If statistical tabulation is the principal purpose of the interviews, this type is a likely candidate. All questions and the order are determined in advance of the interview, and the response categories are also predetermined. Responses include various scales, choices from predetermined lists, and agree-disagree options.

5. Mixture. Any specific interview need not be a pure version of these types; it may be a mixture of conversation,

predetermined topics, some specifically phrased open-ended questions, and some closed questions.

Within these interview formats are questions that range from highly open-ended to closed. The interview literature contains a good deal of advice about the differences and the advantages and disadvantages of each. Neither is inherently superior to the other. If you want the interviewee to have full latitude to structure responses, an open-ended question is preferred. It could be appropriate to ask a job candidate to "Tell me something about yourself." And it also might be appropriate to ask "The date you completed your last degree." For most interviews, a mixture of both relatively open and relatively closed questions is effective.

A behavior to avoid is inadvertently asking closed questions when you want to give respondents an opportunity to share their true feelings or their best thinking. If you happen to be interviewing a person who only answers the question posed, "Are you satisfied with your job?" may not give you much information. "How do you feel about your job?" should give you more. Fortunately, people tend to give you the information you want rather than a precise answer to a question. In any event, we can often recover from a bad question by asking a follow-up. It is better to get it right the first time.

Leading and loaded questions are usually best avoided. Even here, there is no pat answer. Sometimes a seemingly leading question may break down an inhibition or a reluctance to speak openly. Recently I was interviewed by a university official about my reaction to a speaker his office had just sponsored. After giving the purpose for his call he said: "The reason I am asking is that I was somewhat disappointed and wanted to get other people's reactions." My first silent reaction was the thought that he was using bad interview technique. He was telling me his feelings and then asking for mine—an approach that usually biases a response. Later, I concluded that his approach may have been a good one under the circumstances. My tendency, since his office sponsored the speaker, might have been to give a pro forma, patsy response. He was telling me to go ahead and be frank. If you have any criticisms, let me know them. Such a tactic, however, should be used with caution.

An important point to remember in the interview is that the questions in many situations are as appropriate from one person in the exchange as they are from the other. If it is appropriate, the interviewer should be careful to create the possibility for questions to come back. That does not mean to ask at the tail end of an interview whether the interviewee has any questions. That is an often-used courtesy, and not inappropriate, but if a full exchange is desired, more than that is required. The last-minute invitation to ask a question is frequently a notice that the interview is about to end, so it is really a mixed message. The interpretation is likely to be: "Ask me a question, but make it perfunctory because I have to get on to other things."

Questions are the primary stimuli in an interview. There is great variety in how they can be asked. Learning which kind of question to ask and when to ask it is an important part, although not the only part, of the interviewing skill.

*Was there an adequate and appropriate response?* Just as important as the question in an interview is the response. A perfectly formulated question has little value if it does not elicit an appropriate response. Further, answers to questions demand a response in many interview situations. Unless it is purely an information-gathering interview, the two-way relationship should be encouraged.

Both the interviewer and interviewee should monitor whether adequate responses are made and take some action if they are not. The simplest inadequate response is simply not answering the question asked. If the ability to be evasive is a knack you would like to develop, watch politicians respond to questions in a televised interview. If asked a question considered hostile, damaging, or to which they do not know the answer, they use the tactic of answering a different question, one they do wish to answer. As an interviewer, this is a response to learn how to prevent or to get beyond. A common interviewer mistake, particularly if the nonresponsive answer is far afield of the question, is simply to ignore the response and go on to something else. If the question is not worth a probe to get it back on track, it probably is not worth asking in the first place.

One strategy for dealing with an evasive response in a conversational or interview guide format is to go on for a while with other questions and then come back to the evaded one. Something like "Let's get back to X for a minute, I'd like to learn a little more . . ." may get the question back on track. If the answer is still evasive, you have stronger reason to believe the sidestep was not inadvertent. Then, if the question is still important enough to pursue, you have a chance to practice your more advanced interviewing skills.

Probing gives the interview participant a chance to pursue the evaded question, to dig a little deeper to the response to a question answered superficially, and to pursue specific information not volunteered immediately. It gives the interviewer the chance to understand better the feelings and reasoning of the other party. Probing can be very positive for the interviewee as well. Often a person in an interview has information to share, but is reluctant. A line of questioning can help the person tell the story he or she wishes to tell. Probing may be simple. Sometimes "Tell me more about . . ." may do the job; sometimes more-careful and specific questioning is needed.

Interviewers sometimes make simple mistakes that prevent getting adequate responses. One common error is "rescuing" the interviewee. A question is asked to which the person seems to be having difficulty responding. What may be a very revealing moment is lost when the interviewer jumps in with some kind of help—perhaps rephrasing the question or maybe suggesting a line of response the respondent might follow. It almost boils down to the interviewer answering his or her own question. In most cases, this loses the chance for an adequate response.

Stopping short of the payoff answer in a line of questioning is another way to lose response information. Reference interviews over the telephone seem especially vulnerable to this mistake. A personnel officer may call a reference, usually with a list of standardized, open-ended questions. The questions cover the surface characteristics of a job candidate, but often stop there. The respondent in this case usually feels an obligation to be honest in response to questions, but does not feel obligated to volunteer damaging information. So honest and positive answers can be given. A little probing might unearth some weaknesses, but is not done.

A good interview generates adequate responses. The parties involved should assure that occurs; often they do not.

*Were both questions and responses fully heard?* While this is worthy of a separate question on the checklist, it cannot be done well in most interviews unless the first three steps are also done well. Asking initial and probing questions are part of the "hearing" process. Good probes are not possible without at least some of the communication implied in hearing.

This step, to be completed successfully, involves listening, and it also requires capturing or using the information generated. A large amount has been written and said about listening skills over the years. The very common errors are well known, such as interrupting the respondent. That physically as well as mentally prevents the respondent from conveying information to the interviewer.

Other more-subtle barriers can get in the way of really hearing the message. Stereotypes may not only cause an inappropriate judgment about a person, they can shut down your ability to hear what they are saying or feeling (Uris 1988: 70). A stereotype can shut down or alter information before it enters your consciousness. A close cousin to stereotypes is a tendency to make overly quick judgments about people, about their intelligence or personality. Sympathy or empathy (Uris 1988: 73) can also distort perceptions.

Knowing what to listen for is often overlooked in the efforts to teach us to be more open to the feelings and experiences of others. We can be alert to many things, some of which are entirely irrelevant to the task at hand. Clarity about the purpose of the interview is a starting point for knowing what to look for.

Part of the job is receiving the relevant signals from an interview, whether those signals are factual information or perceptions or emotions. Capturing and using that information can be another matter. In some circumstances the purpose of the interview is to reach a decision during the interview itself, a sales interview, for example. Recording information then might be minimal. It might simply be left to memory in casual interviews. In many interviews, systematically recording and processing the information is an integral part of achieving overall objectives. Clearly different situations call for different approaches. Sometimes a tape recording is acceptable (but both parties should know), sometimes note-taking is best, sometimes capturing impressions on paper or dictaphone immediately after an interview is preferred.

## A NOTE ON GROUP INTERVIEWS

Most of the principles that characterize individual interviews also apply to group interviews. The same range of purpose can be served, from seeking information to changing behavior.

One-on-one interviewing is still the most frequently used form of interviewing, but group interviewing for informational purposes is gaining popularity in a number of settings and for multiple purposes. Much of that popularity has come from the discovery that focus-group interviewing can be used for purposes other than market studies (Hambrick and McMillan 1989). Used regularly in marketing studies since the 1950s, the application of the focus-group approach has expanded over the years from marketing to other purposes in business, government, and not-for-profit organizations. These comments about group interview are drawn largely from experience with various applications of the focus-group approach. Group interviews, including those labeled focus groups, are taking on many permutations these days. If reasonable principles are followed, group interviews can be effectively adapted without adhering to a purist approach. Keep the four checklist questions in mind.

One argument for group interviews is simple efficiency—it is possible to get information more quickly by interviewing a group of people than by interviewing each individually. The more-powerful argument, however, is the increase in the quality and richness of information that a focus group can provide. The purpose is to create an environment in which individual group members are stimulated by the perceptions, opinions, and ideas of the other members of the group. In many one-on-one interviews, the stimuli are limited largely to the interviewer's questions. A group interview creates the possibility of one person sparking a response in another, and so on. The overall response thus may be stronger than it would be if those same people were interviewed individually. There is also the possibility of bias and distortion of information. Still, for some purposes, especially where it is important to understand the perceptions of a class of employees or clients, group interviews can be very effective.

Group size in a focus group is typically six to ten. There should be at least one group, and perhaps more, representing each identifiable segment of the population being interviewed. The time required for a focus group interview typically ranges from one-and-a-half to two hours. The setting can be any location appropriate for an uninterrupted small-group discussion. Where focus groups are routinely conducted, a special meeting room is often set up.

If you are interviewing enough people to require more than one group, relatively homogeneous groups are usually arranged so that the interview discussion will result in an in-depth point of view, not an adversarial proceeding filled with argument or conflict. This also helps ensure that individuals will not be afraid to express their feelings about the issue at hand. Homogeneous groups representing other perspectives are interviewed separately. In a study of health-care issues, for example, doctors, nurses, and patients would likely make up separate groups rather than be combined into a single group interview. Part of the planning process, then, is to determine who is to be interviewed and in what grouping.

The group interview itself can be thought of as involving three phases: introduction, in-depth discussion, and wind-down and summary.

The introductory phase should include a brief self-introduction of participants, an explanation of the general purpose of the session, and presentation of the central topic for the session. The introduction of the subject for discussion should lead smoothly into the second phase of the session—the in-depth discussion. The discussion leader typically has several goals:

• frank involvement by participants in the issue at hand;

• participation by all members of the group;

• enough discussion on each point to get a clear understanding of the feelings of participants.

It is important to achieve an open, flowing discussion. Although the leader normally has an interview guide with the points to be covered, there is no required sequence of topics. The leader should not conduct the session simply as a series of questions, which every participant answers in turn. The leader has the responsibility for moving the discussion along and not letting it get bogged down.

Usually, a well-planned focus group session has a rhythm with the wind-down occurring naturally. The points in the interview guide will have been covered, and the group may have begun to repeat ideas raised earlier. The group leader's job is then to bring the discussion to a smooth close, to summarize the main ideas from the group and, if needed, to get final clarification.

The group leader's job throughout the three phases is to provide guidance and assure positive movement of the discussion without heavy-handed domination. The leader also should be sensitive to the group but not be a pushover. Walking this line between being over- and underdirective is a matter of experience, practice, and feedback.

## SELF-DIRECTED IMPROVEMENT STRATEGIES

Interviewing, perhaps more than most generic management skills, is one that can be enhanced through the activities most of us conduct on a daily basis. Being alert to opportunities and then using them is the primary requirement. Several of the learning strategies are based on creative use of what you already do. Give them some consideration and also think of others that use the same principle. Some strategies, though, do require a trip to the library or other extra effort. But they, too, can be worth it.

### Popular Media

The entertainment industry provides one good source of interviewing information. The interview is a very popular format for mass-media entertainment including shows hosted by Johnny Carson, David Letterman, Arsenio Hall, Ted

Koppel, Oprah Winfrey, Phil Donahue, Geraldo Rivera, McNeil/Lehrer, and others.

A political or other debate is often a form of interviewing with two adversaries being interviewed side-by-side.

### Adapt Public Speaking

Developing skill at public speaking and interviewing are mutually reinforcing, with proper adaptation. Interaction, engagement, eye contact, commitment to subject, and energy can all be important parts of interviewing.

### Create Opportunities

Some activities are interview-intensive. One learning strategy is to create opportunities for activities that provide a chance to practice interviewing and to watch others interview. Volunteering to serve on selection and interview committees is one such opportunity. It may be an especially useful experience if a panel approach is used since you can both observe others as well as practice the craft yourself.

### Books

A large body of literature about interviewing is available. Some of it is research based, but more is advice based on the experience of practitioners and consultants. Here are a few worth attention; there are many more.

Bell, Arthur. (1989). *The Complete Manager's Guide to Interviewing: How to Hire the Best*. Homewood, Ill.: Dow Jones-Irwin. Comprehensive guide to employment interviewing.

Cohen, Akiba A. (1987). *The Television News Interview*. Newbury Park, Calif.: Sage. Not a "how to" book, this is a cross-national comparative study of news interviewing for television. Includes an explanation of the similarities and differences between television and other forms of interviewing.

DiGaetani, John Louis, ed. (1986). *The Handbook of Executive Communications.* Homewood, Ill.: Dow Jones-Irwin. A comprehensive book on organizational communications, including several practical essays on interviewing.

Dillon, J. T. (1990). *The Practice of Questioning.* London: Routledge. An assessment of the practice of asking questions in a number of professional settings: classroom, courtroom, psychotherapy and medical clinics, personnel interviews, criminal interrogation, journalistic interviewing, and surveys.

Drake, John D. (1989). *The Effective Interviewer: A Guide for Managers.* New York: AMACOM. Practical advice for the operating manager. Also contains what the author terms the "hypothesis method" for interpreting the meaning of data gathered during the interview.

Eder, Robert W., and Gerald R. Ferris, eds. (1989). *The Employment Interview: Theory, Research and Practice.* Newbury Park, Calif.: Sage Publications. An edited volume, this collection contains twenty-two essays covering a range of topics about employment interviewing: history, the effects of preinterview impressions, the interview as a recruitment device, issues of reliability and validity, and other topics.

Faux, Marian. (1985). *The Executive Interview.* New York: St. Martin's Press. Focuses on the interview process for executives emphasizing leadership and the ability to work with and manage others.

Fear, Richard A., and R. J. Chiron. (1990). *The Evaluation Interview.* 4th ed. New York: McGraw-Hill. Useful chapter on training interviewers. It is a "practical how-to-do it work . . . that spells out detailed procedures for handling applicants from the time they walk into the room until the interview is terminated" (p. xiv).

Goldman, Alfred E., and Susan Schwartz McDonald. (1987). *The

*Group Depth Interview: Principles and Practice.* Englewood Cliffs, N.J.: Prentice-Hall. A relatively comprehensive text on focus-group interviewing as a market research tool.

Janz, Tom, Lowell Hellervick, and David C. Gilmore. (1986). *Behavior Description Interviewing.* Boston: Allyn and Bacon. This book makes the case for behavior description interviewing as the most effective interview strategy for hiring. The core of behavior description interviewing is asking interviewees to describe how they performed in a recent specific situation selected for similarity to one that might occur in the prospective job. "Tell me about the last time you . . ." The book provides detailed instruction for using the approach and offers a variety of examples.

Krueger, Richard A. (1988). *Focus Groups: A Practical Guide for Applied Research.* Newbury Park, Calif.: Sage Publications. Instructional guide for using focus groups for purposes in addition to marketing research.

Mabery, D. L. (1980). *Tell Me About Yourself: How to Interview Anyone from Your Friends to Famous People.* Minneapolis: Lerner Publications Company. This is a book for children and young adults about journalistic interviewing. It has good advice for any interviewer.

Metzler, Ken. (1977). *Creative Interviewing: The Writer's Guide to Gathering Information by Asking Questions.* Englewood Cliffs, N.J.: Prentice-Hall. Written for the journalism field but with ideas useful beyond, the author says the book is an outgrowth of the discovery that "the number one problem of student journalists is interviewing: gathering information by oral means" (xi). The creative interview, he claims, is one that produces a higher level of intelligence than "either participant could produce alone" (10).

Moffatt, Thomas L. (1979). *Selection Interviewing for Managers.* New York: Harper and Row. This is an experience-based practical guide to selection interviewing. It touches on team or board interviews as well as one-on-one.

Smart, Bradford. (1989). *The Smart Interviewer*. New York: Wiley. Focuses on the employment interview. Includes a discussion of rapport building as well as conducting reference calls.

Uris, Auren. (1978). *The Executive Interviewer's Deskbook*. Houston: Gulf Publishing Company. "The manager's job demands mastery of dialogue." With this sentence Uris begins an argument that interviewing is an executive activity that covers a variety of situations, not just the normal personnel function. The book provides suggestions for interviewing in situations that involve encouragement, praise, criticism, performance review, counseling, dismissal, raise requests, complaint handling, meeting the press, and others.

Uris, Auren. (1988). *88 Mistakes Interviewers Make . . . And How to Avoid Them*. New York: AMACOM. This book focuses on common mistakes and means to correct them in organization based interviewing. The eighty-eight faults in the interview were selected on the basis of their frequency and their importance. A sample of the mistakes discussed include: being afraid to probe, fearing the interviewee's silence, being stymied by an evader, and being flustered when you are an interviewee.

Yeschke, Charles L. (1987). *Interviewing: An Introduction to Interrogation*. Springfield, Ill.: Charles C. Thomas. Provides a text for interviewing in the justice field.

## Audio and Video

Interviewing is a topic well suited to capture by both audio and video cassettes. Actual or simulated interviews can be recorded so it is possible to get a relatively full sense of an interview in action. A limitation is that most of the recorded material is about formal interview settings, e.g., an employment interview. Here is a small sample from local libraries. The search strategies suggested in chapter 7 can easily produce a longer list, including items in specialty areas not touched on by these.

Bassett, Glenn A. (1981). *Productive Interviewing: The Problem-Employee Interview.* 2d ed. New York: AMACOM. Part 4 in a series of 5. An audio cassette and accompanying booklet.

Beachman/Silverman Production. (1988). *Interviews, Careers and the Jitterbug Blues.* Washington, D.C. This is a thirty-five-minute color video focusing on careers, composure during the interview, and the actual interview process.

Faber, Don. (1981). *Productive Interviewing: Appraisal and Career-Counseling Interviews.* 2d ed. New York: AMACOM. Part 3 in a series of 5. An audio cassette and accompanying booklet.

Hinrichs, John R. (1981). *Productive Interviewing: The Exit Interview.* 2d ed. New York: AMACOM. Part 2 in a series of 5. An audio cassette and accompanying booklet.

Hinrichs, John R. (1981). *Productive Interviewing: The Information Interview.* 2d ed. New York: AMACOM, Part 5 in a series of 5. An audio cassette and accompanying booklet.

Mitchell, Garry. (1980). *How to Interview Effectively.* New York: American Management Association, Extension Institute. Six audio cassettes and a workbook covering the interviewing process, the psychology of interviewing, legal aspects of interviewing, and the four typical types of personnel interviews: employment, performance or evaluation, disciplinary, and exit.

Professional Training Specialists. (1988). *Interviewing With Confidence: The Complete Guide to Successful Interviewing.* This video is an edited version of a four-hour seminar taped at California State University, Chico, on employment interviewing from the perspective of the applicant.

Valentine, Raymond F. (1981). *Productive Interviewing: The Selection Interview.* 3d ed. New York: AMACOM. Part 1 of a series of 5. An audio cassette and accompanying booklet.

Williams, Jerry, and Walt Slaughter. (1985). *Changing Your Job to Change Your Life.* Idea Marketing, Inc. The video presents aspects of job change as part of career movement. Includes information about the periods before, during, and after the interview.

## CONCLUSION

There are many learning resources in addition to those listed here, and no doubt there are many other ideas for developing and using the skill of interviewing. It is one you should be able to use, formally or informally, on a daily basis. I hope to be better able to find out how far it is to the next village on my next trek in Nepal.

## REFERENCES

Dillon, J. T. (1990). *The Practice of Questioning*. London: Routledge.

Hambrick, Ralph S., Jr., and James. H. McMillan. (1989). "Using Focus Groups in the Public Sector: A Tool for Academics and Practitioners." In *Journal of Management Science and Policy Analysis* 6, no. 4: 43–53.

Henze, Geraldine. (1986). "Interviewing Skills for Managers." In John Louis DiGaetani, *The Handbook of Executive Communication*. Homewood, Ill.: Dow Jones-Irwin. (635–650).

Mabery, D. L. (1980). *Tell Me About Yourself: How to Interview Anyone from Your Friends to Famous People*. Minneapolis: Lerner Publications Company.

Patton, Michael Quinn. (1980). *Qualitative Evaluation Methods*. Beverly Hills, Calif.: Sage Publications.

Uris, Auren. (1988). *88 Mistakes Interviewers Make . . . And How to Avoid Them*. New York: AMACOM.

# 5

## Relating: For Performance and Satisfaction

Two similar units in a large, relatively bureaucratic organization displayed very different characteristics. Each unit had about an equal number of professionals, all quite competent. Unit A was extraordinarily conflict-ridden; every meeting featured bitter debate. Sometimes a decision emerged and sometimes not. When a majority did prevail, the minority often refused to participate in the implementation of the decision. Some relationships outside of meetings were characterized by conflict and others by avoidance. There were factions, tight little groups that talked among themselves but communicated very little to members of other factions. Unit A did not have a clear sense of purpose or direction. Some members were strongly committed to one activity and other members to something else. The situation deteriorated to the point that grievances and lawsuits were threatened.

Unit B was not entirely conflict-free, but conflict did not characterize its functioning. Meetings frequently featured lively debate but ended with agreement that the decision made was legitimate and would be endorsed by everyone. When conflicts did occur, they were resolved and then forgotten, with no bitter residue. Members of Unit B shared ideas and information and assisted each other in important tasks. Suggested ideas, although not always adopted, received due consideration. Although some friendships within the unit were closer than others, they did not affect professional working relationships. A high level of morale and a sense of energy characterized the unit. There was a sense they were going somewhere.

These two vignettes are hypothetical, but they contain elements that most of us probably recognize. Professional relationships can be destructive and bitter, but they can also be productive and positive. What is it that brings about one rather than the other?

Two stories cannot begin to capture the diversity and variety of professional organizational settings. Neither conflict nor energetic cooperation is the salient dimension in many settings. It may be boredom, or individual task commitment, or many others. How members in an organization relate to each other is, of course, not the only factor that determines how it functions, but it is one of the most critical.

Aside from the diversity that characterizes working relationships, there is a multitude of perspectives and roles, making any simple assertions about what is and what is not an effective way to relate to others an impossibility. We relate to superiors and to subordinates, to peers within our organizational niche and peers across various boundaries, to competitors and collaborators (and sometimes one person may be both). We interact with those with whom we share values and those with whom we have serious disagreement. Some of our professional relationships are casual and some are intense. Relating effectively is a demanding skill. There clearly is room for differences of opinion about what is and is not effective behavior in this arena. However, how persons relate to each other is an important determinant of how well the organization functions and how satisfying the professional life is for those who inhabit it. Relationships have a major impact on efficiency, effectiveness, and level of in-

novation of the organization, as well as the emotional health
and vitality of its members.

It is extraordinarily easy for the motives or personality of
one person to be misread by another. Relating is difficult
enough on a one-on-one basis; it may be compounded as
the numbers increase. A group, a "simple" collection of five,
ten, or twenty people working in an office or on a project
team can become truly complex. Such a group can be highly
productive or locked in debilitating conflict; a highly compatible group that interacts regularly inside and outside the
workplace or a collection of loners even during business
hours; a group that can conduct a task-oriented meeting and
get on to other things or one that can spend three hours in
a meeting and not accomplish anything useful.

Relating to each other is a primary feature of professional
and social life. It is a rare professional who works alone.
Even a lonely entrepreneur must interact with others on a
regular basis. For most of us, our own success is dependent
on the quality of those interactions. Many of these interactions are one-on-one, and many are in larger groups. Some
are highly formal in tone, others are informal.

Despite the importance of relating to professional and organizational accomplishment, it is not uncommon for professionals, including managers, to ignore or even resent the
time and effort required in the interaction with other people.
They may say: "I didn't get any work done; all I did was
talk to people all day," or "What a lost day; I did nothing
but go to meetings." In part this is simply a statement that
a lot of other work is still to be done. It often contains two
other messages, though. One is a definite expression of personal preference to spend time alone working on individual
tasks. This message is often conveyed loudly and clearly to
those around and is often interpreted as a lack of interest in
or even rejection of them and their work. The other message
is that we may be handling the relationships poorly. Time

may in fact be spent with other people in nonproductive or wasteful or even destructive ways. "I spent the whole day in a meeting" may mean that nothing was accomplished, not that meetings are in principle a waste. If wasted meetings become a pattern, though, it may become generalized to all.

## ORGANIZATIONS WITH EFFECTIVE RELATIONSHIPS

The following paragraphs summarize my conception of an organization in which members exhibit effective relating skill, both at the one-on-one and group levels. You are invited to develop your own view if it differs from mine. The purpose of this characterization is to establish a conceptual case of an effectively functioning organization or organizational unit from which we can move to a sense of the relating skills required to bring it about.

### Communications

An organization with effective relating skill has a free flow of professional ideas and information. The information exchange is open to all members. Ideas both about the substantive work of the organization and the way it functions are discussed in a participative forum. Alternative viewpoints are expected and encouraged.

### Decision Making

Decisions are made in the organization on a professional basis, not on grounds of personal loyalties, self-aggrandizement, or for other reasons. Professional differences exist and are not suppressed in the decision process. Full and honest discussion helps maintain a core of agreement so that a decision is supported vigorously by those who opposed as well as those who supported it. Decisions are not agonized over. They receive full discussion conducted in an efficient way that moves toward closure. Final decisions are clear and public.

## Energy, Direction, and Supportive Environment

The organization has a certain synergy. The organization as a whole is able to produce more than its members could individually, and each individual is able to do more in the organization than he or she could alone. This sense is shared by each organization member. Although everything is not shared, each member has an interest in the work and welfare of the others. The success of one person is thought to reflect positively on the organization as a whole, and the good work and success of one is appreciated by the others. Each is willing to fill in and help out when others need it. The organization has a sense of energy. There is a feeling that it is going somewhere.

A large amount of responsibility for the effective functioning of an organization rests with its leaders. The recent spate of leadership literature may reinforce the belief that it is the leader who makes the organization succeed or fail. I do not wish to dispute this position; organization leaders are critical. The point I wish to emphasize, though, is that leaders as well as other members of an organization need to exert human-relations skill. It is tough for one to pull it off without the other. It is difficult for an organization leader to mold a high-performance organization if the members express no willingness to learn or to exhibit appropriate relating skills; similarly, it is difficult for the members of an organization to function well if the leaders do not exhibit those same skills. The skills in this chapter are important for people at all levels in the organization. The only difference is perhaps a sense that the higher in the organization a person resides, the greater the responsibility he or she ought to feel to display these skills. Still, don't leave it to the leader. It may be necessary to try make an organization work without an effective leader.

The interpersonal relationships within an organization, of course, could not account for all of the success implied in the description of a high-performance organization. Resources, perhaps authority, and other prerequisites form the foundation without which the relationships would not exist, at least in the same way. Yet relationships can account for much of it; poor relationships certainly could destroy it.

Relating is critically important among the generic skills professionals need to function effectively. Several skills already discussed touch on this one. Public speaking, interviewing, and even writing contribute to establishing human relationships. Those skills can be used and built upon in developing the broader ability for effective human relations. But there is more to effective human relations in the work place than those three skills alone represent.

## MEETINGS AND THE ART OF RELATING

We can use meetings, whether large or small, as a context for viewing some of the many problems and virtues of people relating to each other. In many ways, a meeting is a microcosm of an organization at work. Many of the relationships are brought together and placed on display. Personality traits that otherwise might stay hidden may become apparent in a meeting. This is not to say that all relating problems come out in meetings, or that they only occur in meetings, but it is a place to start.

### Meetings

Billions of salary dollars are spent on executives, managers, and other employees during the time they sit in meetings. Yet the sentiment seems to be that we are not very good at conducting meetings. Dunsing's book (1977) *You and I Have Simply Got to Stop Meeting This Way* struck a chord not only because of the clever title but also because of a widespread negative attitude toward meetings. A recent newsletter for government managers contains an article (Axley 1988) that lists some suggested reasons for poor meetings:

no agenda

key people not in attendance

unprepared participants

domineering leader

personal sparring competition

poor facilities

poor timing

outside interruptions

no decisions or resolutions

Most can be corrected with some commitment and corresponding skill from leaders and participants. Let's examine meetings with an eye to moving them toward the kind of energetic organization described above.

As is the case with interviews, the first question about any meeting may be: Is it necessary? Many are not. However, the only thing worse than too many meetings may be too few. Meetings are part of the glue that holds an organization together. It may be the only time some people see each other and the only time they interact about anything of importance.

So the fantasy of eliminating meetings is not likely to be realized. Still, eliminating a few may be all right. It is more than a waste of time when a needless or wasteful meeting is called. Especially for highly task-oriented persons, the waste tends to damage rather than build relationships with others, especially those responsible for causing the waste.

If you cannot eliminate meetings, you can make them better. If my view is correct that meetings are reflections of the organization in action, making this effort to improve them should be considered important enough to warrant a significant expenditure of energy. Meetings, rather than being a drag, can be a key force in giving an organization vitality and direction. In many organizations, they do just that.

Effective meetings, like all other aspects of an organization, require effort, and, in most organizations, they also require changed behavior from leaders and participants. Neither can do it alone.

### Leader Behavior

Here are a few ideas that leaders might consider in moving toward a more energetic and effective organization.

1. Don't call a meeting if there is nothing important to be accomplished by it. If a memo will do, use it. If it is time for members to socialize, throw a party. Sometimes a meeting purely to share information is appropriate. In a professional organization and with an increasingly educated workforce an information meeting should be called only if some form of interaction with the "messenger" is needed. With complex information, this is sometimes required. If training is the purpose, it should be so designated.

The primary purposes for meetings should be problem solving or decision making. Those functions deserve the time of organization members.

Corollaries of the principle of not calling unnecessary meetings are not to cancel one that is needed and making sure that it is scheduled if needed.

2. Get feedback from participants. The leader's job is a tough one, so there is no reason to jeopardize it by trying to go it alone. An actual feedback form asking participants for an evaluation of occasional meetings is one way to do this.

I know leaders who have gotten useful perceptions and ideas from doing just that. There are other ways.

3. Manage the meeting. This means lots of things and may vary with context, so a comprehensive list is not possible here. Some important items are these:

—Start on time and quit on time. Little is quite as irritating as showing up on a busy day on time for a meeting and the chair waits for all the stragglers. A few meetings in which important business is underway before they arrive will send a message to the habitual late-comers. The point is not to be a hardnose or worse for its own sake. The idea is to create the conditions for an energetic organization. Such an organization has busy people, so their time should be respected. Busyness does not mean the lack of cordiality; it does mean respect for others.

Ending a meeting on time is done for the same reason. Active people schedule their time. A positive sign that an organization is an energetic one is a meeting that runs forty-five minutes past the announced adjournment time and nobody stays to the end.

—Have an agenda and stick to it. This does not mean that full and open discussion should not occur. In fact, that should *be* the agenda. A rambling series of discussions unrelated to the agenda is not simply a waste of time, it leads to poor decision making. Effective decision making requires focus.

—Control dominating members and assure the opportunity for less-vocal persons to contribute. The evidence is clear on this point; the most-vocal members do not always have the most-important input or make the wisest decisions. Not only for the morale of the organization but also for more effective decision making the leader needs to assure all have an opportunity to contribute.

4. Record decisions. If meetings are for problem solving and making decisions, it is imperative that solutions arrived at and decisions made be remembered. Usually that means recording them in some fashion. For most purposes, a sim-

ple record of decisions is adequate; any more than that gets in the way. That is why an outside note-taker or a recording is usually not effective. Each tends to produce more information than is needed and it gets in the way. A meeting chair should record decisions or see that it is done. This applies to two-person meetings as well as larger ones.

5. Follow up. Make sure that decisions made are acted upon.

### Participant Behavior

Participants also have an important role to play if the organization's human relations are to work effectively in a meeting setting.

1. Be on time. To be late is to say to others that your time is more valuable than theirs. Such a message does not help develop effective relationships.

2. Avoid digressions. This too is based on respect for other people.

3. Use good speaking skill. Make a meeting an effective interactive speaking performance, not a monologue. Even use visuals or go to the flip chart if it will help make a point.

4. Be assertive. Don't let some error or a position you strongly oppose go unchallenged. Effective relationships cannot be developed in an organization if members are silent when something can be done and complain in hallway whispers when it is too late.

5. Listen. Be sure to hear what other people are saying. The interviewer's skills should be put into practice. That may mean asking questions. It does mean making sure you understand the position of the other participants. It does mean listening rather than formulating your next attack.

6. Do not use the meeting to attack or take pot-shots at others.

## Meetings as Practice Field for Relationships

Much more could be said about meetings and the good and bad behavior that goes into them. They are a practice field for human relationships and a place where relating skills can be observed and used.

## Specialty Techniques for Improving Meeting Relationships

A standard meeting format does not always produce the kind of interactive relationships desired for problem solving or decision making. A number of specialized group processes have been developed to help overcome some of the relating problems that regularly occur when groups get together to make decisions. Following is a brief examination of two techniques: nominal group technique and brainstorming. Both have a strong track record when used properly; both on occasion are abused.

## Nominal Group Technique

The nominal group technique (NGT) is one of the most versatile methods available for focusing the thinking of a group of people on a problem. Its rationale includes two key points. First, it gives all members of a group an equal opportunity to have input rather than running the risk of some people being squeezed out by the group process. It virtually forces everyone in the group to contribute. Second, the NGT process results in a decision about priorities. The most important or useful ideas are identified and ranked as the principal product of the NGT. There is multiple input, which is moved toward a consensus.

## Uses of NGT

The nominal group technique is often used as a means to structure a single meeting. It is also possible, however, to string several NGT sessions together in response to different phases in the decision process. Using the NGT, a group could develop a better understanding of the problem(s) being found; then in a new session, identify and assess the importance of goals; and still later, generate and evaluate program or policy ideas. The same group might be involved in each of these stages, or a different group could be used in each stage.

The technique allows considerable variation in group size and composition. However, these should be given careful consideration to assure that your purpose is effectively served. From a process point of view, a seven-to-ten-member group is ideal. However, five to fifty or more can be accommodated if your organizational needs call for it. If more than fifteen are involved, they can be broken down into small groups and the small-group results consolidated. Group composition, of course, depends on purpose. It might be made up of clients, staff members, or others.

Time required for a single NGT session ranges from around one and one-half to three hours. The setting for an NGT session can be almost any place away from distractions, where individuals can write and flip-chart sheets can be taped to the wall. If the group will be large, find a location suitable for breakout groups of seven to ten each.

The materials required to conduct a session include flip chart(s) (at least one for each group), markers, masking tape, writing paper, pencils, and 3″ × 5″ cards.

The NGT is made up of a series of small, distinct steps.

1. Preparation for session and assembly of group.

2. Introduction of the subject and purpose to the group.

3. Silent idea-generation by all participants.

4. Round-robin recording of ideas from group members.

5. Group clarification and discussion of each item.

6. Individual listing of the top five items on 3″ × 5″ cards and ranking of these items.

7. Recording of individual rankings on flip chart and tabulation of group rankings.

8. Discussion of group ranking.

9. Repetition of steps six to eight if desired.

*Preparation.* Like any activity, the quality of an NGT session will be improved by thorough preparation. Preparation includes organizational matters like arranging a meeting room, getting the necessary supplies, and contacting participants, as well as substantive matters like determining the focus and scope of the session and the composition of the group.

*Introduction of subject and purpose.* The first step is to present clearly the problem or issue being addressed and the purpose of the session. Ideally, the focus of the session can be expressed in a question written out and displayed in front of the group throughout the process. It can be written on a flip-chart sheet, at the top of individual worksheets, or both.

*Silent idea-generation.* Group members are now asked to write key ideas in response to the focus question presented. Members are encouraged to write on worksheets brief phrases that come to mind in response to the question. This is to be done silently with no interaction between members of the group. (This is where the term *nominal group* originates. At this stage, at least, it is a group in name only, a noninteractive group.) Group members are encouraged to write as many ideas as they can. This is a critical part of the process since most of the final product is based on what is generated in this phase.

*Round-robin recording.* After the silent idea-generation is concluded, each member's ideas are recorded on a flip chart visible to the whole group. The recording is done in round-robin fashion. The leader/recorder asks for one idea from one group member and then proceeds around the group, giving each person an opportunity to present one idea. Each idea is numbered or lettered serially and written on the chart. As a page is filled, it is torn off and taped to the wall so all ideas remain visible.

The round-robin recording goes around until all ideas are recorded. Members are encouraged to provide an idea each round; but the leader should make it comfortable for them to pass if they have exhausted their ideas. Also, individuals should be encouraged to "hitchhike." If an item offered by someone else stimulates a new idea on their part, they should offer it. If someone else has presented an idea on an individual's worksheet, he or she can cross it off, avoiding duplication on the master list.

*Group clarification.* After all ideas have been recorded and displayed, the next step is to discuss each idea in turn. Short discussion is allowed for each item, carefully moderated by the group leader to assure approximately equal time for each item and avoid long arguments about an individual idea. The discussion should:

- clarify each item to assure that all participants understand its meaning;
- clarify the reasoning behind the idea; and
- expose opinions about the idea but without extensive argument.

*Individual ranking.* After the discussion, individuals are asked to provide their own ranking of the items the group has generated. This can be done by giving each participant five 3″ × 5″ cards. They are then asked to rank these five cards from most important to least important. The number 5 is written on the card with the most important item and 1 on the least important. (It is critical not to reverse this scoring and assign 1 to the most important.)

*Recording of rankings.* Take a break after these ranking cards are completed and collected by the group leader. During the break, the group leader can record the rankings on the flip-chart sheets, add the numbers, and determine which are the top-ranking items.

*Discussion of group ranking.* The tabulated ranking is now presented to the group, and the group leader can facilitate a brief discussion of the voting pattern. This discussion should be defined as clarification, not pressure for anyone to change votes. The discussion may examine inconsistent voting patterns and provide for an opportunity for further discussion of items group members think received too few or too many votes.

*Revote.* The process may be stopped after one ranking; however, voting, discussion, then revoting produces a more accurate reflection of thinking and preferences than does a single vote. Thus, you might want to repeat steps six through eight to reach the final product of the group.

Although the nominal group technique is not appropriate for all occasions, it offers a number of advantages in many situations. The NGT offers a definite structure for conducting a problem-solving meeting and thus avoiding a rambling and unproductive process. It gives all participants a chance to contribute and still produces a consensus or a record of where the group stands, and it provides a definite stopping point.

### Brainstorming

Brainstorming is most frequently associated with creativity and idea generation. There have been many adaptations of brainstorming as well as many misconceptions. One of the misuses of the term is to treat it as a meeting with no structure. To the contrary, effective brainstorming is a carefully planned and structured process. Conducted well, it can be very helpful in generating useful ideas and making a preliminary evaluation. It can create a low-threat environment in which even the most reticent participant is willing to contribute.

The basic notion is to develop the largest possible number of ideas about a given issue. The larger the number of ideas, the greater the likelihood there will be some good ones. Of course, numbers alone are not the objective. Efforts are made to stimulate thoughts that normally would be suppressed.

A key point in brainstorming is to reduce inhibitions so that it is socially acceptable, even encouraged, for participants to generate and share what otherwise might be considered dumb ideas. In a brainstorming atmosphere, the unusual idea is encouraged and rewarded. Although brainstorming can be used spontaneously when a group is meeting, it is generally recommended that a session be well thought out in advance.

Five to fifteen participants make a good group size, but the technique's flexibility allows variation. Time for a full-fledged brainstorming session can range from forty-five minutes to over two hours. The idea-generation stage itself may range from fifteen minutes to an hour or more.

The setting for a session should be one in which participants can be comfortable, away from distractions. There should be room for two flip-chart stands, and it should be possible to tape flip-chart sheets to the wall.

Five steps are involved in a classic brainstorming session. At the conclusion of a good session, you should have one or more ideas of immediate usefulness, one or more ideas worth further exploration, a lot of ideas that cannot be used, and perhaps a new way of looking at the problem.

*Preparation.* Like the nominal group technique, preparation for brainstorming involves logistical matters, like the meeting room and supplies (see above), and substantive matters, like type of participants and statement of the problem to be addressed. The session should focus on an issue of importance to the organization but allow enough latitude to encourage innovative ideas.

*Warm-up session.* This step is frequently left out, but it can add considerably to the effectiveness of the idea-generating process. The warm-up can familiarize participants with brainstorming, redirect their attention away from matters not related to the session, help them shed inhibitions, and create the nonjudgmental atmosphere necessary for idea generation. Further, if it is a group that has not worked together, the warm-up period helps participants become comfortable with one another.

This step might consist of two parts. The first could be a brief presentation and discussion of brainstorming rules and procedures; and the second, a five- or ten-minute idea-generation exercise on a topic totally unrelated to the main business at hand. This can be something silly or farfetched, such as, "What uses can you think of for a bunch of old ties that are out of fashion?" or, "How would our society be different if the automobile had never been invented?"

*Idea generation.* The idea-generation phase is, of course, the heart of the brainstorming technique. A goal is to get many ideas flowing in an uninhibited, high-energy atmosphere. A single individual can serve as the group leader and recorder in this phase; however, it is usually more effective to have one or two recorders in addition to the leader. I prefer two recorders who alternate recording ideas on a flip chart, with a page taped to the wall as soon as it is full. With only one recorder, the session may drag waiting for the recorder to catch up.

Four rules guide the conduct of the session, and it is the leader's job to make sure that all participants are aware of them:

• No evaluation will be done during idea generation.
• Many ideas are desired.

- Thinking should be wild, creative, free-wheeling.
- Piggybacking or hitchhiking is encouraged.

The need to suspend judgment, especially the subtle forms such as snickering or rolling eyes, is critical. No evaluation of any kind of any idea should occur during this period. The leaders should be aware that it is very difficult for some people to refrain from expressing judgment, so he or she should be prepared to nip it in the bud if it begins to occur.

Many ideas, including unusual ones, are desired. There are two important reasons for encouraging wild and impractical ideas in a brainstorming session. First, until an idea is evaluated, you cannot tell whether or not it is practical, and concern about practicality will keep good ideas from being thought at all or expressed to the group. Thus, potentially useful ideas will never get generated. Second, bad ideas are useful. That is, a totally impractical idea may lead to a very useful idea. For this reason piggybacking or hitchhiking is encouraged. A participant is encouraged to take someone else's idea, build on it, turn it around, or adapt it.

In most idea-generating sessions, there is a lull at some point. Do not assume that a lull means the group is out of ideas. Often the biggest spurt of ideas comes after a two- or three-minute silence. Do not let a lull signal the end of the idea-generation phase prematurely; do not let the session go too long. Stop the session before the group has run out of steam.

*Categorization and evaluation.* After a good idea-generation session, there should be a large but disorderly list of ideas. In this form the list is not very useful; it needs to be sorted and culled. A set of usefulness categories could be

- ideas that clearly can be used,
- ideas that may be usable with adaption and further development,
- ideas that are not usable.

This preliminary categorization may be all that is required of the group, or further steps may be helpful. In some cases it may be appropriate for the group to arrive at a definite decision or to assess the merits of each group of ideas.

One simple process for categorizing is to place the entire original list where it can be seen, then work with a blank flip-chart. Write the categories on the chart and have the group suggest where items fit, with the recorder listing them by number, or a number and a brief phrase.

Brainstorming remains one of the most effective and versatile methods for addressing a problem situation. It can be especially effective when the full process is used and when its management is treated carefully. It can be an effective means to generate productive interaction in a group in a way that encourages participation by all. It provides one model in which participants do not criticize or ignore the ideas of colleagues, a behavior found quite often in other types of groups.

These two techniques, nominal group and brainstorming, were designed to counter some of the problems in the way people relate to each other in groups. A least for some purposes, they impose a structure that encourages more effective relationships. For example, the nominal group technique assures everyone an opportunity to participate in group deliberations, and brainstorming alleviates the tendency to inhibit the thinking of others. There are other structured as well as informal ways to achieve these and other important objectives in the way we relate to each other. Developing skill at relating can be a real multiplier of your own effectiveness, especially in an organizational setting.

## SELF-DIRECTED IMPROVEMENT STRATEGIES

Relating, or human relations in the workplace, is such a broad topic that it is both easier and more difficult to identify learning strategies for it than for the other skill areas.

### Role Model or Mentor

If you are fortunate enough to identify a person who exhibits a high level of skill in relating to other people in the workplace, you have a valuable, ready-made learning resource.

### Group Training in Interpersonal Relations

Over the years a number of approaches to teaching interpersonal relations in group settings have been developed. These include transactional analysis, interaction analysis, assertiveness training, and others. Workshops on topics like these are regularly available.

### Outdoor Experience

Business, government, and nonprofit organizations are using outdoor adventure as a group learning and team-building approach. Most areas of the country have challenge courses (often called "ropes" courses). Instructors are usually available. Relating in small groups is the central feature of this program.

### Books

Block, Peter. (1987). *The Empowered Manager: Positive Political Skills at Work.* San Francisco: Jossey-Bass. Shows how those who toil in the middle levels of an organization should and can have an impact on the mission and culture of the organization. How to relate to allies and enemies, superiors and subordinates, those within and outside your own unit, is part of his discussion.

Brightman, Harvey J. (1988). *Group Problem Solving: An Improved Managerial Approach.* Atlanta, Ga.: Georgia State University. Focuses on group problem solving. Discusses how managerial teams function, why they fail, and strategies for improving team effectiveness.

Carnes, William T. (1980). *Effective Meetings for Busy People: Let's Decide It and Go Home.* New York: McGraw-Hill. Examines meetings thoroughly and provides keys to successful ones. Touches on a variety of meeting situations and treats the role of a good participant as well as that of chair.

Cole, Robert E. (1989). *Strategies for Learning: Small-Group Activities in American, Japanese, and Swedish Industry.* Berkeley: University of California Press. A comparative study of employee workgroups in three cultural settings.

Cooper, Cary L., ed. (1982). *Improving Interpersonal Relations: A Guide to Social Skill Development for Managers and Group Leaders.* Englewood Cliffs, N.J.: Prentice-Hall. Includes an article on each of four types of small-group experiential training: transactional analysis, interaction analysis, assertiveness training, and the T-group approach. Also contains a chapter that compares and evaluates the approaches.

Dunsing, Richard J. (1978). *You and I Have Simply Got to Stop Meeting This Way.* New York: AMACOM. Concludes that while "most meetings range in quality from poor to horrid," there is hope. Describes changes both leaders and participants can make to achieve better run meetings.

Jackson, Dale E. (1988). *Interpersonal Communication for Technically Trained Managers: A Guide to Skills and Techniques.* New York: Quorum Books. Develops an approach for professionals and managers to improve communication skills whether in a meeting, on the telephone, or during the presenting or the listening side of the exchange.

Kirkpatrick, Donald L. (1987). *How to Plan and Conduct Productive Business Meetings.* 2d ed. New York: AMACOM. Provides advice about how to manage every aspect of a meeting, from preparation to evaluation. Has chapters on problem-solving meetings, instructional meetings, sales meetings, teleconferencing, and others.

Miller, William C. (1987). *The Creative Edge: Fostering Innovation Where You Work.* Reading, Mass.: Addison-Wesley. Describes methods for bringing out creativity and innovation in individuals and groups. Discusses the possibility of institutionalizing innovation in the workplace.

Schein, Edgar H. (1988). *Process Consultation: Its Role in Organization Development.* 2d ed. Volume 1. Reading, Mass.: Addison-Wesley. Focuses on the role of the process consultant in organization development. Provides a useful discussion of how groups form, how they work, and how individuals within them relate to each other.

Schwartzman, Helen B. (1989). *The Meeting: Gatherings in Organizations and Communities.* New York: Plenum. A sociological, cultural, and historical look at meetings and their importance. Less about conducting meetings than understanding them.

Wood, Julia T., Gerald M. Phillips, and Douglas J. Pedersen. (1986). *Group Discussion: A Practical Guide to Participation and Leadership.* 2d ed. New York: Harper & Row. Discusses the role of small groups in decision making and the process of decision making within such groups.

## KEY QUESTIONS

A few questions worth reflecting about in pursuing this topic are these:

How can collaboration be made to work?

How can conflict be kept in bounds and even made constructive?

What are the ingredients of interpersonal communications?

When is teamwork important and how can it be brought into being?

What is effective assertiveness and how can it be developed?

How can a group work together effectively even if it is not a team in any deep sense?

How can misunderstanding and squabbles caused by lack of communications be prevented?

How can you work as a participant in a team?

How should you participate in a meeting?

How should you run a meeting?

How can you prevent a group from stifling your initiative and your self-confidence? The initiative and self-confidence of others?

How can you assure the participation of all members of a group?

## REFERENCES

Axley, Stephen R. (1988). "Toward Productive Meetings: Advice From the Firing Line." *Virginia's Executive Management Letter* (March): 1–2.

Dunsing, Richard J. (1978). *You and I Have Simply Got to Stop Meeting This Way*. New York: AMACOM.

# 6

## Computing: The Contemporary Multipurpose Tool

Even those who so far have avoided using computers are about to be overtaken by an avalanche of them. Computers are too powerful, too cheap, and too convenient not to become a regular part of the administrative and professional workplace. If not already, you are likely to become a convert soon. Even though computers are common in the workplace, there are still many managers and professionals who have not begun to use them as a tool in their own work. Perhaps some would find no advantage in their use, but many could profit from adding computer usage to their repertoire of skills. Others may have learned to use the computer for a few things, but could profit from an expansion of their skill. This chapter is intended to be useful to four types of readers:

- those who have not yet begun to use computers.
- those who have learned one or two applications, but have reached a plateau and are no longer progressing with their computer skill.
- those who are moving ahead with computer skills but would like new ideas or perspectives about learning more.

• those who are already expert, but are looking for ideas to help others learn (recognizing that most skilled computer users are also informal tutors and teachers).

## A FEW THOUGHTS ABOUT THE USEFULNESS OF COMPUTER SKILL

I was relatively slow to become a regular computer user, but now find myself in the convert camp. Just a few experiences confirmed their value for me. In 1985, I prepared a rather lengthy report for a local government. At the time I was not using a word processor so I followed the write-it-longhand, cut-and-paste routine, and then had someone else type it. At the time there was a clerical shortage in the office, so I had to find typing help anywhere I could. Writing the report was fairly demanding; getting it typed was a hair-pulling experience. It became an exercise in planning, inter-departmental cooperation, interpersonal relations, persuasion, and exasperation. Two years later, I wrote a very similar report, but had learned to use a word processor and portions of a graphics package in the meantime. I drafted the report on the computer, which was easier than handwriting and cut-and-paste, and when I finished writing, there was only some formatting and cleanup to do before printing the final report. A good deal of work and frustration was avoided.

Stories about how computers have saved work and made products more accurate, attractive, and useful are plentiful. They come from all kinds of people and organizations. A city council uses a spreadsheet program and an overhead projector (LCD) to keep a running total during a budget work session. A university fund-raising office uses a database program to target and personalize solicitation letters. A student remembers the agony of getting the footnotes to look right on the page and marvels at how easy it is with a word processor. And many more.

Personal use of a computer can drastically cut the lead

time on many projects. (Put another way, it allows procrastination.) You can wait until the last minute and still prepare quality overheads for a presentation or prepare a letter
right before it has to go into the mail. (The procrastinators
and the very busy can think of many more examples.) Procrastination is not required, however. The computer provides a very handy way to start working on a project well
in advance. As soon as you agree to give a speech to the
civic club you can jot out some notes, and then add to it
whenever an idea occurs to you. Of course you don't need
a computer to do that, but it can help. Writing is hard work.
Anything to make it easier can be a good investment.

Working out a budget for a proposal or developing a
business plan for an office can be made a lot easier with a
computer spreadsheet program. It is especially helpful when
you are trying out different ideas. Recalculating even a small
budget can become tedious after a time or two.

The point is not to imitate the salesman's hype, however.
Life was pleasant before the microcomputer, and it can still
be without one. And there are some drawbacks and complaints. Some persons are irritated by "personalized" letters
that they know are mass produced. Rather than producing
a paperless office, the computer industry has probably increased the amount of paper that passes through your mailbox and across your desk. Despite these and other complaints, computers are here to stay and will have an increasing
impact on our lives. The professional who resists making
computer usage one of his or her skills is imposing a hand-
icap on personal productivity and perhaps career success.

## BARRIERS TO AND INCENTIVES FOR
## GETTING STARTED

Getting started is the toughest part of many new en-
deavors, including learning a new skill.

Learning how to learn is a central theme of this entire

book, but it may be especially important in the computer field. The reason is that most professionals will learn several new systems during the course of their careers as well as expand the range of things they can do with a computer (Schrodt 1987). Part of this new learning will come about because the industry is changing; partly it will be a result of individual job changes involving a move to an organization with a different computer environment. Learning the second system (or program) *is* easier than the first, so this prospect of continuing learning should not be troublesome. Further, the direction of the industry is toward more and more "user friendliness." A major dimension in which companies are competing is ease of use for the buyer or end-user.

In comparison with the other skills discussed in this book, computer skill has advantages and disadvantages for those who want to develop or improve it. An advantage is that computers have many of the characteristics of a toy; they can become a focus of attention in leisure as well as work. A disadvantage is the image that using a computer is complex. A second disadvantage is that developing skill in using computers is like shooting at a moving target; the field is changing rapidly.

For those persons with the "right" temperament, the toy-like characteristics of computers are a strong attraction. In a literal sense, of course, computers can be used as a toy or competitors in a game. My first direct encounter with a computer was playing tic-tac-toe on a time-share system as an undergraduate. The computer faculty used the game to entice students to become familiar with the machine. Some stopped with tic-tac-toe, but others began to tinker and do much more. By the end of the semester, some were composing music with the computer. Unfortunately for my computer skill development I then moved to a university that had a much less "friendly" computer environment—one requiring punching and sorting cards. I quickly reverted to UCOWAN behavior (Use a Computer Only When Absolutely Necessary) only to be rescued by microcomputers.

Using a computer literally as a toy, however, does not exhaust the toylike feature. It contains a seemingly endless stream of new features and applications. Learning a little may start an exploration and learning process that becomes a permanent activity. For some people, computer tinkering rivals golf as a riveting pastime.

The sense of complexity that surrounds a computer is a clear disincentive for some people. There are many sources of this perception. One, of course, is that computers in fact are complex. The good news is that most users can ignore that complexity, because user friendliness is an important focus of the computer industry. (This, however, does not mean that you should wait until it is possible to converse with a machine using ordinary language before beginning to use one.) If machine complexity is not a challenge you enjoy, make user friendliness the primary criterion in selecting the system you learn.

The "moving target" nature of the computer industry can be discouraging. Almost any computer will be obsolete shortly after you acquire it. And the same applies to software, an exceedingly dynamic field. Conventions in the English language also change over time, but at a barely perceptible pace. For some users this rapid change is exciting and one of the reasons for being so active as a practitioner of the computer art. For others this brings on a sense of frustration. One colleague longingly wished for one word processing program to be declared standard and then not allowed to change for twenty years.

Whether developing computer skills looks inviting or foreboding at the moment, the issue is whether or not such skills will be useful. Will the payoff exceed the cost? If the decision is to go ahead and learn (or increase) computer skills, secondary questions may be whether to purchase your own, and if so which hardware and software to acquire.

In contemporary society we are all computer users whether we want to be or not. We are indirectly users when we order a Big Mac, make a plane reservation, or call to find out why the utility bill is so high. More directly, we are users at the bank's automatic teller machine (ATM) or at the "card catalog" at many libraries. The question here is whether it is worthwhile to become a more active user. It is worth keeping in mind that being an active user is only a step or two from using the ATM.

### Which System to Learn

One barrier to getting started with computers is the wide range of available choices. It appears that there are so many different hardware systems and so many software programs that just making a wise choice about which to use is a lifetime task. Indeed, there is a lot to choose from, but the choices need not be overwhelming. Two important decision rules can help narrow the search for the appropriate hardware and software.

*Criterion A: What works best?* That can be divided into two questions: Which system has the most power? Which system is the easiest to use?

*Criterion B: What do others with whom you associate use?* (Of course, if you strictly work alone, this may not matter.) This criterion may be more important than the first; it is certainly not trivial. If there is an established computer environment in your workplace, even if you do not use it, that may be the determining factor. Even if your primary interest is personal use of the computer at home, there may be a number of payoffs to acquiring and learning a compatible system. For one thing, there may be people at work who can provide advice and assistance. (One of the nice things about the computer world is that most people enjoy "teaching" what they know.) For another, after developing some computer skills, there may be opportunities to use them at work.

If you work regularly with other people on matters that might involve computer use, word processing for example, having compatible systems and skills is very useful. Information can be shared, drafts can be moved back and forth, and so on. Giving up a little technical power to make the system compatible with those around you may be a good idea.

In most government and business organizations, the hardware of choice is IBM and IBM-compatible machines. In a December 1987 survey among local governments (ICMA 1988), IBM or IBM clones make up 76 percent of those used in the chief executive's office. UNISYS and Apple or Macintosh were next, but far less common. Clearly, in this environment, IBM is most likely to be compatible. Of course even here a particular organization or area might not be in the majority. Even if you work in local government, what might be important is not what is used nationally, but what is used in your particular organization.

The most common software programs reported in the ICMA survey are Lotus 1-2-3, WordPerfect, WordStar, and dBase.

What do you use now? What could you use if you had the equipment and the software and the skills?

### What, If Anything, Should You Buy?

If you have access to a computer, buying one may simply be a matter of convenience. Some people wouldn't be without one (or more) at home. If you have a TV at work, would that mean you do not need one at home (and I do know people who have no TV at home)? For some, that attitude is a little overzealous; for others, it is just the way it is. But the person who has made the computer a regular tool may go even further as indicated by this quote from a computer magazine editorial (Patchett 1990: 5): "I often need to use a computer at unexpected times, and the ability to carry one that is small enough and light enough to be a permanent part of my briefcase contents is a major advantage. Have you ever been caught in a situation where you could have used a computer but didn't bring yours with you because it was just too inconvenient? Chances are you have."

## AN ORIENTATION TO HARDWARE AND SOFTWARE

This chapter cannot serve as an instruction manual, but a brief orientation to a few concepts may be helpful. Skip the next few pages if you are already a user just looking for some learning strategy tips.

### Operating Systems

The categories of software of importance to the user are operating systems and application programs. The operating system is the overall manager of what the computer does. From the user's perspective it is a good administrative assistant who, with minimal instructions, takes care of a variety of logistical and communications tasks. The operating system provides the connection between the machine and the specific program you are running. It is helpful to think of the computer working at two levels. Level one, the operating system level, provides the structure to move from one program to another. It is the point of contact when the machine is first turned on or when the user moves from one type of activity to another. Most of the functioning of contemporary systems is not visible to the user, meaning that it is necessary for most of us to learn less and less (the administrative assistant is taking care of matters so we won't have to bother).

In today's microcomputers, three operating systems are most likely to be used:

*MS-DOS.* IBM and IBM-compatible machines typically use DOS (disk-operating system). These use typed-in commands, e.g., *DIR,* which prompts the computer to list a directory of files.

*Visually Oriented Systems (VOS).* Made popular by the

Macintosh, visually oriented systems are becoming more common. These use a mouse and symbolic pictures as the means of entering commands.

*UNIX.* An operating system developed by Bell Laboratories for mainframe computers, but adapted for micro use as well. It has more sophistication than DOS or VOS, but is more complex to use.

### Application Software

Application software is the second level; it provides the payoff. The application software manipulates the words or calculates the numbers and presents them in a variety of formats. There are literally thousands of off-the-shelf software packages available, and more coming all the time. Word-Perfect, dBase, and Lotus 1-2-3 are among the most common in business and government offices. These generic packages can be used in virtually any office setting. There is also more-specialized software for specific settings, like attorneys' offices, dental offices, government organizations, and so forth. The International City Management Association *Software Reference Guide* 1990 contains 758 software programs ranging from "Cemetery Management System" to "Sanitel," a program to monitor wastewater treatment plant operations. Custom software can also be written, but is less frequently required as more and more off-the-shelf packages become available.

*Word processing.* For most users, the biggest payoff, or at least the most common use, of a computer is for writing. What can a computer do for you? Primarily two things: it can allow you to produce a quality document even if you are not an accomplished typist, and it can allow you to write and revise more easily. A typewriter makes a direct connection between the user's key stroke and ink on the page. After the key is hit, it is too late to take it back. All the fancy whiteouts, erasing fluids, and erasable paper could never quite cover up the results of a spastic finger stroke. The computer does not put ink to paper until you get it right (or at any intermediate draft stage). So, the final copy shows none of the errors that actually occurred during production. For speed, typing skill is still nice to have. For a perfect final copy, typing skill is not required.

The easy revision word processing provides alters the very process of writing (see the chapter on writing). With pen and paper and with a typewriter, the mechanics of writing urge, although they do not literally require, a linear process. A writer would tend to start at the beginning of whatever is to be produced and work through it to the end. A draft might be produced, perhaps with a number of holes to be filled in later, for alteration, correction, and retyping. Composing with a word processor is much more "organic" (Schrodt 1987: 36). The writer may, without penalty, begin at any point. Future writing sessions may also focus on any part of a manuscript. The writer may bring up the document on the screen, page through it, making corrections and changes, and stop anywhere to write new text. Chunks of text can be moved or deleted with little effort. And a clear result of that change can be seen immediately.

Although the computer cannot cure all of the problems of writers, it can alleviate some of them. One result of being penalized for a writing mistake using pen or typewriter is the tendency to "pre-edit"—to try out mentally several versions of something you want to say before writing the first word. The penalty for changing your mind is so low with a word processor that early versions can easily be tried out on the screen (Foster and Glossbrenner 1983). This may not eliminate writer's block, but it may minimize it. One of Hollywood's images—that of a frustrated writer surrounded by crumpled sheets of paper—has virtually become obsolete. The writer may still be frustrated, but the crumpled paper is already beginning to look quaint.

Let's walk through some of the features of word processors with two ideas in mind: What might you look for in a word processing package when deciding which one to learn or to buy? What expectations should you have about what to learn and what you will be able to do with a package?

Most word processors use the "what-you-see-is-what-you-get" (WYSIWYG) format, meaning that what you see on the screen is what will be printed in hard copy. There may be some modest differences, so hard copy needs to be checked to assure that it turned out as intended. Basically though, what you see on the screen is a good approximation of the paper product. An alternate, and far less common, system is one in which formatting commands are imbedded in the text and are not "obeyed" until the document is printed. This requires the user to estimate what the printed product will be. This is not difficult for frequently used commands, but it is still usually necessary to print a hard copy or two and make changes before the format is right.

While working with a document, the writer can only see what is on the screen, about twenty-four lines. A good word processor, though, has a variety of ways to move about in the text. After some skill is developed, it is much easier to move through a text with the computer than it is with hard copy. You can move a letter at a time, a line at a time, screen by screen, page by page, to a particular page, to the location of a particular word, and other variations.

The wraparound is another feature of most word processing systems that eases the writing process. In typing, the writer must decide when to end a line and move to the next. The word processor makes this decision for you when the length of the word goes past the line length. This is one less thing for the writer to think about.

Especially for the person drafting a document, the most appreciated feature of the word processor is the ability to make changes in text. Several features make this easier than other ways of getting words from brain to paper. The word processor is usually in "insert" mode when it is called up.

Beginning with the typing of the first letter, the insert mode is in operation. After text is entered, the insert mode becomes one of the word processor's powerful revision tools. New text can be inserted anywhere in the text simply by moving the cursor to that location and typing (with some systems an insert command is necessary). As you type, existing text will be pushed ahead, making room for the new material. This works equally well whether you are inserting a single letter or space or a whole sentence, paragraph, or chapter. Most systems also have a typeover mode; this allows you to have the new text replace, letter by letter, the old. This feature can be turned on or off. (Don't forget to turn it off when done. Otherwise you may inadvertently replace text instead of inserting.)

A companion feature is the ability to "cut and paste," to move a block of text. As a pencil and paper writer before becoming a word processor user, I had developed a regular routine and good skill at cutting and pasting (actually cutting and stapling in my case). So the text-movement feature of the word processor became an instant favorite. The process is quite simple in most word processors: mark the beginning and end of the text to be moved, then place your cursor at the new location and press the *enter* key. The exact keys for carrying out this sequence vary from package to package, but the process is quite similar among most.

Formatting is another feature, or set of features, a good word processing system provides. These features include centering headings, allowing underlining, boldface, and in many cases, italics. Depending on the printer used, some allow various print (font) sizes, multiple columns, shading, and other features. These formatting features in word processing are pushing toward rivaling the graphics capability of desktop publishing packages.

The "search" and "search and replace" functions on a word processor can be very helpful in working with a document. A search will allow you to find the occurrence of a particular word, phrase, or subtext up to some maximum. This can be a helpful way to move quickly to a section of a text if an idea strikes that you would like to insert. It is not necessary to remember that the word *entropy* is on page 47. Let the computer search for the word *entropy*, or chapter 3, or any other modestly distinctive identifier. The "search and replace" enables you to replace a word or subtext throughout the document. All replacements can be done automatically, or you can set it so that you are asked for permission at each occurrence of the item to be replaced.

Either built into a word processing program or as add-on programs, grammar and style checks are available to analyze your prose. They will highlight phrases and word usages that violate rules or conventions. Included in many are measures of "readability," essentially a count of big words and long sentences translated into the level of schooling required to understand them. Also included are flags that the language may be sexist. And of course violations of other rules are flagged—dangling participles, overuse of passive voice, and all that. Of course the writer is free to ignore all of the computer's advice, and much of it should be ignored.

A spelling check feature is an important (indispensable) attribute of a good word processing system. Even for good spellers, misspelled words can creep into a text. Most brains are not well equipped to find all of these buried errors. At best it is a tedious chore. A spelling checker matches all words in a text against a list of words. If there is no match, a word is listed, sometimes along with a list of similar words, as suggestions for the word you may have intended. You may then choose one of the suggestions or retain the word you originally inserted. The spelling check is only as good as the list of words in the program's dictionary. Many proper names, slang, and technical jargon may not be included. But it is possible to add words to some programs, and it is also possible to get a spell checker especially designed for certain technical fields, medicine, for example. A spelling check, however, will not eliminate correctly spelled but misused words. It will not catch "I eight two much on Thanksgiving." So the need for proofreading is by no means eliminated.

*Desktop publishing.* While the primary purpose of word processing is to produce manuscript, albeit clean and neat, the intent of desktop publishing programs is to produce fancy copy, often with illustrations, ready for printing. While word processing replaces the typewriter, desktop publishing replaces the typesetter, or serves the same function. Desktop publishing can combine text, graphics, and creative page layout for professional-quality brochures, newsletters, reports, and even books.

Word processing and desktop publishing have grown closer together, and it is sometimes hard to tell one from the other. More-sophisticated word processing programs can produce multiple columns, use fonts of different sizes, and incorporate simple graphics. Desktop publishing programs can insert and edit text and some even have spell checkers and other text development aids. Still, there is a division between the two, and the standard procedure is to develop text on a word processor and transfer (import) it to a desktop system for page layout and graphics.

Desktop publishing programs, like word processing packages, come with varying degrees of sophistication and cost. They are designed for publishing professionals as well as amateurs at a club or office that produces an occasional newsletter or brochure.

*Spreadsheet.* The manual equivalent of the computer spreadsheet is an accountant's ledger pad and the many variations it can have. The spreadsheet has many uses in addition to budgets and projected sales. It can be used to record and keep a running average for student grades, keep a checkbook, and many other tasks in addition to massive computational problems. The key feature, among many others, is the instant recalculation of all related figures when one is changed.

A blank spreadsheet on your computer monitor looks something like the following:

|   | A | B | C | D | E | F |
|---|---|---|---|---|---|---|
| 1 |   |   |   |   |   |   |
| 2 |   |   |   |   |   |   |
| 3 |   |   |   |   |   |   |
| 4 |   |   |   |   |   |   |
| 5 |   |   |   |   |   |   |
| 6 |   |   |   |   |   |   |
| 7 |   |   |   |   |   |   |
| 8 |   |   |   |   |   |   |
| 9 |   |   |   |   |   |   |

*Data base management system (DBMS).* While the spreadsheet corresponds to the accountant's ledger pad, the database management system is the electronic equivalent of the filing cabinet. These two programs have some features in common, but their strengths and basic purposes are quite different. The spreadsheet is best used for numeric calculations; the database management system is best for storing, updating, and retrieving information. A simple use for a DBMS is a mailing list. Names, addresses, and other information can be stored, then updated, and retrieved. Depending on how the data base is set up, retrieval can be by many different factors: by name, by identification number, by income, date of last transaction, just to name a few. The DBMS can also be used to eliminate duplication.

*Graphics packages.* Computers these days turn out graphics that a few years ago would have required a graphic artist (and the money and lead time required). Presentations, whether written or oral, can be given a professional look with relative ease, and if used well can communicate more effectively. That is the good news. The bad news is that professional graphics are becoming much more common so it takes more for a product to stand out. Graphics capacity is built into other packages, like spreadsheets, and in separate specialty packages.

*Statistics packages.* A spreadsheet program and a database management system are capable of producing some statistical computations. If you have specific statistical needs or require a fairly high degree of sophistication, a dedicated statistics program may be desirable.

*Specialty programs.* The growing list of specialty programs truly provides a range of choice for both professional and personal purposes. A quick scan of the advertisements in a computer magazine or the products in a software store is indicative of what is available.

flowcharting software

tax preparation software

forms-creation software

English to Spanish translation software

legal software (for producing legal documents)

time and billing software

grammar, writing style, and punctuation checker

tutorial software (to teach software)

personal finance tracking and management

form fill-out software

project management software

computer diagnostic software (for detecting computer problems)

investment and portfolio management software

accounting software

time management and appointments scheduling

audiovisual presentation software

golf lessons

The above list is from ads in a newsstand magazine. Literature in specific professions includes reference to other specialized software. For example:

college admissions, financial aid, and registration

student housing

conference scheduling

competency-based instructional planning

course development software

### Adding a Modem

A microcomputer by itself is dependent on the user for information. You may supply it through the keyboard, by using diskettes from some other source, or with the use of a scanner if you have one. The addition of a modem opens up a range of information sources. Simply, a modem is a device to translate computer codes to a form that can be transmitted by telephone line. It can be used to connect your computer to a more powerful computer or to sources of information. More and more organizations are setting up database systems that allow access through a computer connection. A few examples with more in the next chapter:

*Library "Card Catalogs."* It is possible to search the holdings list of many libraries from your own computer with the use of a modem and a telephone connection.

*Online investing.* Charles Schwab, among others, allows clients to get market prices and place investment orders through their own computers.

*Newspapers and journals.* Several services offer online access to the text of a number of journals and newspapers.

*Local government information.* A system for accessing information about how localities have solved various problems.

*Census data.* Access to census data.

*Legal databases.* System that contains federal and state legal cases and statutes.

*Training.* Online listing of upcoming conferences and workshops.

*Bibliographic searches.* A number of online services for bibliographic search are available.

*E-mail.* One of the most popular uses of a modem, or hard-wired system connecting terminals, in many offices is an E-mail or electronic mail system. Users dial into a central computer that serves as a mailbox for different people. Unlike telephone conversations, the recipient of any E-mail message does not have to be attentive or present while the author of the message is sending it. Rather, the recipient signs on and checks for messages when it is convenient. Most active E-mail users get in the habit of checking and responding to their E-mail messages once or twice a day, just as they check their regular mail. E-mail systems often have a reply function so that immediately after reading a message, typing the word *reply* automatically directs the response to the recipient's account. E-mail allows subordinates to approach more easily superiors in the chain of command since it is less formal and more conversational in character than an official memo. E-mail also allows memos to be sent out to a large group at once, making it easier to arrange meetings and projects that require consensus.

*Networks.* Networks are just a giant E-mail system across locations sometimes thousands of miles apart. One such network is BITNET, a system that connects mainframe computers at different universities around the country and world. NSFNET and INTERNET are two other university-linked networks; CompuServe is a network for general users. Networks linking institutional mainframes allow a user in one location to communicate from a personal computer without a long-distance phone charge. Then the message can be directed via the network from the mainframe in the sender's location to the mainframe in the receiver's location. The receiver can later sign on from a personal computer locally or hundreds of miles away and check for network messages. Replies may be returned in similar fashion. Files and manuscripts can be sent through the network enabling near-instant exchange on co-authored work.

*Uploading and downloading files.* As E-mail and networks become more important, harnessing the power of the mainframe from your own personal computer also increases in significance. To do so, files must be easily transferred from your PC where they are created, entered, and/or modified to the mainframe where they may be analyzed and/or directed to recipients. Most institutional mainframes have software to allow this type of file transfer. Uploading means transferring a file from your PC operating system to an appropriate location on the institutional mainframe. Downloading means reversing the process and transferring a file from the mainframe operating system to your PC operating system.

## SELF-DIRECTED IMPROVEMENT STRATEGIES

"Hands-on" is the best way to learn about and improve skill at computing. This applies at the early as well as more-advanced stages. The machine tends to be quite resilient, so there should be no concerns about making mistakes. The machine may lock up, but don't panic. Just turn it off and start over. It is not elegant, but even advanced users resort to this tactic. A beauty of hands-on learning with the computer is instant feedback. If it works, you receive positive reinforcement immediately; if it does not, it will let you know, usually in a nice way. It is like learning whitewater canoeing. If you make a wrong move you most likely will know it quickly. At least the negative feedback learning to use the computer is not cold and wet.

### For the Apprehensive: Slow and Easy

Assume that you have decided to join the world of computing but do not want to plunge in. Your prefer to begin cautiously, with uncertainty about the use you wish to make of it. You may or may not be apprehensive about getting involved with this machine. Some people are. I was in the computer lab one evening and noticed a woman sitting in front of a terminal just looking at it. It had not even been turned on. Two days later, she came in again and did the same thing. After a few minutes I diplomatically asked if she needed any help. She said she was taking an evening studies class and had unexpectedly been given a small computer assignment. She had never touched one before, and had a severe case of apprehension.

For the apprehensive or just for a person in no big hurry, here is a list of strategies.

1. Subscribe to *PC Novice,* a magazine targeted for beginners.

2. Visit several computer stores and just browse.

3. Take a word processing short course.

4. Try out a friend's computer.

5. Subscribe to *PC Today.*

6. Decide on software.

7. Buy (or otherwise gain access to) a computer.

8. Start playing with it on a regular basis.

9. Take a short course or workshop on occasion as a way to move forward.

10. Continue reading and using the machine to keep up.

### Plunge

Perhaps it fits your personality better to start in a hurry with a burst of enthusiasm.

Option A. Do a quick search, buy a computer and some software. Use the manual, one of many instructional books, or a videocassette to learn to use the system.

Option B. Take a course.

Option C. Take a new job that requires you to use a computer.

Option D. Find friends (make sure they are good ones) with computers and hang out at their houses.

Option E. All of the above.

As a general rule, it is usually better to have a human being help in the early stages of becoming acquainted with computers. The complex-appearing hardware and the several instructional manuals tend to be confusing if not intimidating. As one person said after a fair amount of learning time: "I now know enough to read the manual."

### Upgrading

Perhaps you are already a computer user, but have stalled out at a level lower than you would like. You can learn word-processing at a level adequate for drafts or even clean copy of letters and papers or other documents, but remain at a very low skill level. Necessity may create enough pressure to learn a new trick every now and then. Even necessity, though, may simply cause you to solve a particular problem by brute force without bothering to learn how to use the power of the application program.

*One-a-week program.* A simple strategy for continuing on an upward learning curve is to develop a list of specific computer skills—four or five or a dozen. Whatever comes to mind. Put them in some order and then set a schedule for learning one a week (or day or month). As you become aware of new skills that it would be nice to learn, add them to the list. These may be relatively small matters, like learning to use the spell check function, or the table of contents feature.

On occasion though you may want to take a bigger step, for example, acquiring, installing, and learning a new applications program. You can break this down into once-a-week steps or find a larger block of time to get started and then move back to the smaller-step, once-a-week program.

Building this kind of systematic structure for learning is important. The tendency for many people, and perhaps professionals are more susceptible than others, is to keep fully busy with what needs to be done so the "I'll do it when I get time" items never get done. The once-a-week structure, if taken seriously, puts the development of computer skills on the needs-to-be-done list.

### RESOURCES FOR COMPUTER LEARNING

Computing is big business. The size of the market for computers and the many associated products is dependent on the knowledge level of potential users, and just about everybody is considered a potential user. As a consequence, the marketplace is filled with products for making us computer-literate. And, of course, there is money in that too. In an earlier chapter we commented about the number of books about improving writing. The literature about writing, or at least the current flow, is miniscule compared to the literature, and other products, about how to compute. There are dozens of magazines, newsletters, books, training manuals, videocassettes, instructional computer programs, and more. The field is filled not only with products that provide instruction on specific topics, but also a steady stream of innovative devices and techniques for providing that instruction. The steady and growing stream of information is a real bonus—except it appears overwhelming. The magazine rack with a dozen computer magazines can appear more intimidating than enlightening. A guide to the search can be helpful. One simple framework is to think of the computer literature as fitting into one of the following cells:

| Content | *Novice* | *Level of Knowledge* *Intermediate* | *Expert* |
|---------|----------|--------------|--------|
| General | | | |
| IBM Specific | | | |
| Mac Specific | | | |
| Application Specific | | | |

## Popular Magazines

Popular magazines are one of the best learning tools available since the field is changing so rapidly. There are magazines for different skill levels and almost every specialty area. Here is a list I found on the magazine racks at a couple of bookstores. There are more.

*Compute*

*Computer Shopper*

*Macworld*

*PC LapTop Computers Magazine*

*PC Magazine*

*PC Novice*

*PC Today*

*PC World*

## Manuals

Most bookstores have several shelves full of manuals for the popular software packages. Some are 600-page tomes and others are much less detailed "quick reference" documents.

### Workshops

There is an abundance of workshops at varying levels of sophistication. They range from an hour or so to several days in length; from free to very expensive.

### Computer-Based Tutorials

The computer is an instructional tool. So there is every reason to use the computer as an instructional tool to teach the use of computers. Tutorials in almost all of the popular commercial software packages are available. One company's recent magazine ad, for example, listed tutorials for Lotus 1-2-3, DOS, WordStar, dBase IV, WordPerfect, MultiMate, and Pagemaker.

### Videocassettes

Instructional videos for many software programs are available. Set up a VCR and TV next to your computer and follow the video instructions. (You can use a portable VCR/TV in an office to provide instruction to new employees or to increase the skill of current employees.)

### User Groups

User groups provide a good way to develop and improve computing knowledge and skill. Most are organized around hardware or software, e.g., Macintosh Users' Group or Lotus 1-2-3 Users' Group.

### Books

The literature on computers is growing so rapidly that a library is far less useful as a source than it is for other topics. By the time a typical library orders, catalogs, and then puts on the shelf a manual for WordPerfect 5.0, version 5.1

has been released. So computer books about specific packages or technologies may best be sought elsewhere; libraries are still useful for more generic material, such as the impact of computerization on the workplace. The list below is suggestive of some books with at least modest staying power.

Brent, Edward E., Jr., and Ronald E. Anderson. (1990). *Computer Applications in the Social Sciences*. Philadelphia: Temple University Press.

Daiute, Colette. (1985). *Writing and Computers*. Reading, Mass.: Addison-Wesley.

Dvorak, John C. (1989). *PC Crash Course and Survival Guide*. Rockville, Md.: Scandinavian PC Systems.

Foster, Timothy R. V., and Alfred Glossbrenner. (1983). *Word Processing for Executives and Professionals*. New York: Van Nostrand Reinhold.

Garson, G. David. (1987). *Academic Microcomputing: A Resource Guide*. Newbury Park, Calif.: Sage Publications.

Kroenke, David M., and Kathleen A. Dolan. (1990). *Business Computer Systems: An Introduction*. 4th ed. New York: McGraw-Hill.

Norris, Donald F. (1989). *Microcomputers & Local Government*. 3d ed. Washington, D.C.: ICMA.

Ravden, Susannah, and Graham Johnson. (1989). *Evaluating Usability of Human-Computer Interfaces: A Practical Method*. New York: John Wiley & Sons.

Schrodt, Philip A. (1987). *Microcomputer Methods for Social Scientists*. 2d ed. Newbury Park, Calif.: Sage Publications.

Sullivan, David, J. Wesley Sullivan, and William L. Sullivan. (1989). *Desktop Publishing: Writing and Publishing in the Computer Age*. Boston: Houghton Mifflin.

Williams, Frederick. (1989). *Computer-Assisted Writing Instruction in Journalism and Professional Education*. New York: Praeger.

## REFERENCES

Foster, Timothy R. V. and Alfred Glossbrenner. (1983). *Word Processing for Executives and Professionals.* New York: Van Nostrand Reinhold.

International City Management Association. (May 1988). *Microcomputer Use in the Local Government Administrator's Office.* MIS Report 20:5.

International City Management Association. (1990). *Software Reference Guide 1990.* Washington, D.C.: ICMA.

Patchett, Craig. (1990). "Editorial," *PC LapTop Computers Magazine* 2:11:5.

Schrodt, Philip A. (1987). *Microcomputer Methods for Social Scientists.* 2d ed. Newbury Park, Calif.: Sage Publications.

# 7

---

# Searching: Putting Modern Technology to Work

Today's informational world is rapidly expanding. More and more information is generated in more and more specialized areas. In this environment, the capacity to efficiently find relevant information, for purposes of solving a specific problem or simply maintaining currency in a specialty area, is important for managers and professionals. Subscribing to a few journals in our field does not now provide adequate contact with the rapidly expanding world of information.

A few numbers are indicative of the information explosion. One source (Granick, Dessaint, and VandenBos 1990: 286) reports that between 6,000 and 7,000 articles are published daily in over 40,000 journals. The legal records in the United States now contain more than 3.3 million cases and 30,000 a year are added. The U.S. Congress produces 700,000 pages a year, and 70,000 new patents are issued each year in the United States. The list of large numbers easily could be expanded. The information explosion is a cliche, but it is also reality.

Fortunately, corresponding with the information explosion are advances in the technological capacity to organize, store, and retrieve information. Large amounts of information can be stored, and retrieval, increasingly, can be pin-

Note: Virginia Cherry is the principal author of this chapter.

pointed. Online computer searches enable retrieval organized by author, subject, subfield, key word, and others. Search output can be in the form of bibliographies, abstracts, full texts, and more.

The search process may be simplified by an intermediary, a librarian or a computer search specialist, who can assist with the process of identifying and retrieving material. It is usually not effective to turn the entire task over to someone else. The online search process is an interactive one that requires a stream of decisions. If an intermediary is used, the search is best done jointly so you can make the critical substantive decisions. The trend, however, is away from the use of assistance toward end-user searching (Granick, Dessaint, and VandenBos 1990: 294). Both technological advances and the proliferation of vendor services are pushing in the direction of do-it-yourself searches.

Some managers and professionals are competent in the use of manual and computer search systems; many are not. General lack of familiarity with search techniques recently was made apparent by a group of successful middle-level managers on campus for a weekend seminar. They were given an assignment to find two or three current articles about a topic of their own choosing and report back on what they had found and how they had gone about the search. An approach several used was to walk around in the library stacks where bound journals are shelved looking for journals with *management* or a related word in the title. When found, the table of contents was scanned for an article on the chosen topic. Some even chose the topic based on an interesting article that happened to appear in the first journal they happened to find. Clearly, this is a blunt information search and retrieval system.

## THE SEARCH ACTIVITY

The search activity can be a systematic process. Search strategies in this chapter are those to use in obtaining as much information on a topic as needed in as little time as possible. A quick search is often necessary, and these strategies will save time.

The importance of a systematic process is threefold: First, the searcher is able to become familiar with the primary and secondary sources in order to obtain an overview of the field; second, the searcher is able to utilize the full range of materials that are available for use; and third, a systematic search results in a wise use of time. Therefore, a knowledge of indexing and abstracting services, government documents, and journals as well as how to use them can be critical in the search process.

Seekers of information, whether lawyers, doctors, city managers, or corporate executives, can acquire expertise and ease in the search process and become proficient in scanning the literature. Strategies for retrieving information are vital to any successful manager.

## SEARCH STRATEGY 1: KNOWING YOUR RESOURCE COLLECTION AND ITS SERVICES

The first strategy for obtaining materials is the determination of resource collections to which you have access. In the past, businesspeople have relied upon nearby academic or research libraries. People living in a large metropolitan area had access to these extensive collections usually at a small fee, if any. They had the capacity to retrieve through elaborate interlibrary loan networkings any material not available within the collection. They also utilized online database searching services at very low costs. Cities also had specialized sources of information within state agencies.

Although research and university libraries still remain primary sources, they are not the only sources in the search for answers. More and more corporations as well as small businesses are developing their own libraries or information centers. Professionals are turning to in-house systems as well as their personal computers, recognizing the importance of up-to-date knowledge. Decisions need to be made rapidly, and there is little time to depend upon outside sources such as the university or public library. Also, due to fiscal restraints and increased costs for materials and services, libraries are no longer offering information retrieval at low cost or no cost.

Whether the collection is in-house or outside, the searcher needs to become familiar with the basic pattern of organizing or arranging the materials within a collection. All collections or libraries maintain a similar arrangement in organizing their materials:

1. Card catalog or online catalog: the guide to the collection.
2. Reference materials, including up-to-date directories, handbooks, dictionaries, encyclopedias, and bibliographies: these core publications are important for current information.
3. Indexing and abstracting services: the section serving as the guides to the contents of journals and periodicals.
4. Government documents: publications printed by the Government Printing Office or generated by local, state, or federal governments.
5. Professional journals and periodicals.
6. "Stacks": section of books that may circulate. These materials are shelved by subject areas.

When using a collection for the first time, request a tour or talk with the collection's manager in order to learn the arrangement and any special services offered. Collections share materials through interlibrary loan or cooperative sharing services and offer online database searching.

## SEARCH STRATEGY 2: LEARNING TO USE THE GUIDE TO THE COLLECTION

Once you are familiar with the services of the collection as well as the location of materials, determine what is available within the core of the collection. Every collection, whether large or small, has a guide to the contents of the collection.

Libraries traditionally used card catalogs for listing the contents of their collections. These were 3″ × 5″ index cards filed alphabetically in card trays. Access to the collection was through three entries: author, title, and subject. Card catalogs are no longer used in many libraries today, although the card catalog is still used in small or specialized collections.

## SEARCH STRATEGY 3: SEARCHING THE ONLINE CATALOG BY SUBJECT, AUTHOR, AND TITLE

Today, many card catalogs have been replaced by the online catalog. These online catalogs use a monitor and keyboard with access to the collection in traditional author, title, and subject entries.

Entering "A" followed by an author's name will display all publications written by that *author*.

For example:

A—Rabin, Jack

will display:

Rabin, J. (Ed.) (1988). *Handbook of Resource Management.* New York: Dekker.

Entering "T" followed by the *title of the book* will display that publication and its location in the library.

For example:

T—Technology in Banking

will display the following item:

Steiner, Thomas. (1990). *Technology in Banking: Creating Value and Destroying Profits*. Homewood, Ill.: Dow Jones-Irwin.

Entering "S" followed by a *subject* will display all items in the collection pertaining to that subject.
For example:

    S—Marketing

will display many items including:

Gross, Charles, et al. (1987). *Marketing: Concepts and Decision Making*. St. Paul: West Pub. Co.

## SEARCH STRATEGY 4: SEARCHING THE ONLINE CATALOG USING KEYWORDS

In addition to searching the online catalog by author, title, and subject, searching has been enhanced with the addition of "K" or "KW," keyword searching. This is a way of combining keywords in a logical-search statement. A keyword is a significant word from a subject, title, or author. By connecting a subject with an author, you can obtain all materials on a particular subject written by an author. Instead of searching an entire subject area, the search can be narrowed to those materials in a subject area by one author.
For example:

K—Urban Institute and Productivity (Combining *publisher* and *subject*)

will list:

Greiner, John. (1981). *Productivity and Motivation: A Review of State and Local Government Initiatives*. Washington, D.C.: Urban Institute Press.

K—Sonnenberg and Marketing (Combining *author* and *title* word)

will list:

Sonnenberg, Frank. (1990). *Marketing to Win: Strategies for Building Competitive Advantage in Service Industries.* New York: Harper Business.

Keyword access also uses the addition of symbols or words to connect words in order to narrow or broaden the search. Thus, an individual keyword or a combination of keywords can be used to form a search statement.
For example:

The use of "and" as a connector:
K-Marketing *and* Productivity will list all publications relevant to both of these two terms.

The use of "or" as a connector will broaden the term:
K-Marketing *or* Productivity will list all publications relevant to either/or marketing and productivity.

The use of "not" as a connector will narrow the term:
K-Marketing *not* Productivity will list all publications relevant only to marketing excluding those also relevant to productivity.

*"Nesting"* of keywords is another search strategy. For example, entering the search statement, "K-Marketing and (Private or Public)," will retrieve all items on marketing relating to both the private and public sectors.
Audiovisual materials may also be searched within the collection by using specific symbols. These symbols are displayed either on the monitor or in a "usage" pamphlet available for the user and vary by vendor. For example, NOTIS Systems, Inc. uses F.FMT., DT1, S. fmt. symbols in

searching for audiovisual materials, journals, magazines, or periodicals and in searching time periods.

K-Marketing and F.FMT. (F.FMT. symbolizes audiovisual item)

will list the following item:

*Marketing Nonprofit Corporations.* (1983). Sunrise, Fla.: D.E. Visuals. (79 slides).

Other useful searching techniques are searching by date and searching for journals, magazines, or periodicals. To limit your search by date, for example,

K-Marketing and 1989.DT1

will display only those items published *during or after 1989.* To search for journals an example is:

K-Marketing and S.fmt.

will display only those journals, magazines, or periodicals relevant to marketing.

## SEARCH STRATEGY 5: SELECTING SUBJECT HEADINGS

When using the online catalog for *subject searching,* you can locate all of the materials in a collection on one topic or subject area. However, online catalogs use controlled subject headings; that is, they are standard subject headings. The searcher must select from the provided subject headings.

In order to select the appropriate subject heading, online catalogs use either *Library of Congress Subject Headings* or the *Sears Subject Headings.* Both of these subject headings are standard or controlled; that is, the researcher must select from the subject headings provided. For example, if the search is "productivity in government," the subject searched must be "government productivity."

Subject headings are listed in the three-volume set of *Library of Congress Subject Headings*. (U.S. Library of Congress. Subject Cataloging Division. 12th ed. [1989]. Washington, D.C.: Library of Congress.) These volumes are usually located near the online catalog.

The subject headings as prepared by the Library of Congress use abbreviations to narrow or broaden a subject search. These abbreviations, UF, NT, BT, SA, and RT are defined below:

UF indicates that the term is reciprocal or synonymous

NT indicates a narrow term

BT indicates a broader term

SA indicates "see also"

RT indicates a related term

For example, in searching for "health planning," the following terms are listed:

UF—Comprehensive Health Planning (synonymous term)
  Health Care Planning (synonymous term)
  Health Services Planning (synonymous term)
  Medical Care Planning (synonymous term)

BT—Medical Policy (broader term)

RT—Health Services Administration (related term)

NT—Environmental health planning (narrower term)

The *Library of Congress Subject Headings* use subject subdivisions under the main divisions. Four categories of subdivisions are generally recognized: topical, form, chronological, and geographical. Topical subdivisions are used under main headings to limit the search. When using the online computer (or card catalog), for example, S-Finance (that is, the subject being searched is "Finance," a main subject heading) will display the following subdivisions:

Abstracts

Bibliography

Bibliography—Indexes

Bibliography—Periodicals

Book reviews

Case studies

Collected works

Computer programs

Data processing

Decision making

Dictionaries

Handbooks, manuals, etc.

History

Law and legislation

Mathematical models

Periodicals

Statistical methods

Study and teaching

Terminology

This is a partial listing of the more than 100 subdivisions within the Finance subject. The online catalog will seek publications from within each category. For example, a search of all "dictionaries" will be retrieved by selecting the subsection "dictionaries."

## SEARCH STRATEGY 6: FAMILIARITY WITH SHELVING OF MATERIALS

Books are shelved by call numbers selected from the Library of Congress Classification System or the Dewey Decimal Classification System. Schools and public libraries use the Dewey system, while university and research libraries use the Library of Congress system. The Library of Congress (LC) system consists of twenty-one major sections, with each section symbolized by a letter of the alphabet, while the Dewey system assigns numbers to materials. Below is a partial listing of the LC system:

A—General Works

AE—Encyclopedias

AG—Dictionaries

AI—Indexes

AN—Newspapers

AP—Periodicals

AY—Yearbooks, Almanacs, Directories

H—Social Sciences

HA—Statistics

HB—Economic Theory

HD—Industry and Management

HE—Transportation and Communication

HF—Commerce

HG—Finance

HM—Sociology

HT—Urban Sociology, Cities and Towns, Regional Planning

HV—Social and Public Welfare, Criminology

J—Political Science

JF—Constitutional history and administration, Civil Service, Government, Administration

JS—Local Government

K—Law

KF—Law of the United States

L—Education

Q—Science

R—Medicine

S—Agriculture

T—Technology

Z—Bibliography

A useful and easy-to-use guide to the LC system is United States. Library of Congress. Subject Cataloging Division. (1978). *LC classification outline.*

The Dewey Decimal Classification system is listed below:

000—Generalities

100—Philosophy (and related disciplines)

200—Religion

300—Social Sciences

400—Language

500—Pure Science

600—Technology

700—Arts

800—Literature

900—Geography, History

Dewey, Melvil. (1979). *Dewey Decimal Classification and Relative Index.* (19th ed.). Lake Placid Club, N.Y.: Forest Press.

## SEARCH STRATEGY 7: KNOWING THE LIMITATIONS OF THE ONLINE CATALOG

The online catalog does not include the vast source of government documents available. Libraries now use CD-ROMs to access the publications of the Government Printing Office by author, title, subject, and keyword entries.

## SEARCH STRATEGY 8: USING ALL THE INFORMATION IN THE CARD CATALOG OR DISPLAYED ON THE ONLINE MONITOR

Just as the card catalog gives important information, the online catalog displays on the screen the same bibliographic information. For example, Jack Nilles's *Exploring the World of the Personal Computer* will display the following information:

Call number: QA76.5 .N553

Author: Jack M. Nilles

Title: Exploring the World of the Personal Computer

Edition: First

Publisher: Prentice-Hall

Place of Publication: Englewood Cliffs, N.J.

Copyright date: 1982

Note: Includes bibliographical references and index

Tracings: (subject headings)
          Minicomputers

Tracings refer to subject headings; useful to note for checking other materials under these subject headings.

## SEARCH STRATEGY 9: USE OF BIBLIOGRAPHIES IN THE SEARCH: A TIME-SAVING TOOL

When using the online catalog, search for bibliographies in your subject area; they will save you time. Bibliographies may be single publications or compiled in collected works.

Bibliographies pull together books and journal articles on broad or narrowly defined topics. For example:

*Bibliographic Index; A Cumulative Bibliography of Bibliographies.* (1937– ). New York: Wilson. A subject guide to bibliographies published, both journals and books.

Blaug, Mark. (1978). *Economics of Education: A Selected Annotated Bibliography.* 3d ed. New York: Pergamon.

Ellison, Frederick, and Jane van Schaick. (1984). *Legal Ethics: An Annotated Bibliography and Resource Guide.* Littleton, Colo.: Rothman.

Lipstein, Benjamin, and William J. McGuire. (1978). *Evaluating Advertising: A Bibliography of the Communications Process.* New York: Advertising Research Foundation.

Sheehy, Eugene, ed. (1986). *Guide to Reference Books.* 10th ed. Chicago: ALA. Includes an extensive listing of handbooks in all subject areas. This is the most comprehensive listing of reference books available.

## SEARCH STRATEGY 10: USING INDEXES AND ABSTRACTS TO SEARCH MULTIPLE JOURNALS IN LESS TIME

The value of indexing and abstracting services is that they compile all journal or magazine articles under one listing. These are accumulated annually, and many are accumulated in five- or ten-year supplements. The table of contents of each journal is compiled for you. For example, all articles written on personnel management are compiled in one subject listing.

An index is usually arranged alphabetically with subject and authors interfiled, while abstracting services are arranged by broad subject headings. An abstract contains a brief statement about the article or book cited.

Indexing and abstracting services also use a standardized and controlled vocabulary with an extensive cross-reference system. Just as the Library of Congress has its own controlled subject listings, so do indexes and abstracts. Main headings appear in boldface capital letters followed by subheadings. Several of the subdivisions used are:

Bibliography

Mathematical models

Research

Statistics

Study and teaching

Training

They use *see* and *see also* to cross-reference the contents. For example:

"See" refers to synonymous terms
PRODUCTION COSTS, *See* Costs, Industrial

"See also" refers to related subjects
PRODUCTIVITY
*See also*
    Efficiency, Administrative
    Efficiency, Agricultural
    Labor Productivity

There are hundreds of indexing and abstracting services available. Listed below are a few of the major services used as well as keys to searching each of them:

*ABI/Inform.* Journal articles to over 400 periodicals in management and administration in business. Search by subject and keyword access. Updated monthly.

*American Statistics Index.* Statistics published by agencies of the U.S. government. Search by title, subject, agency report number, and geographical location. Annual with monthly supplements.

*Book Review Index.* An index to books reviewed in over 300 journals. Search by author and title of book. Bimonthly.

*Business Index.* Over 500 business periodicals and 1,000 general-interest and legal periodicals in the business field. Books and government documents also included. Subject index available on computer output microfilm only. Updated monthly.

*Business Periodicals Index.* An index to over 290 English-language periodicals in accounting, advertising, banking, communications, economics, finance, insurance, labor, and management. Search by subject headings. Monthly except August.

*Criminal Justice Abstracts.* Abstracts of criminology and criminal justice literature. Search by six subject headings. Quarterly.

*Current Contents: Social and Behavioral Sciences.* A "Tables of Contents" format of more than 1,300 journals in social and behavioral sciences covering economics and business. Weekly.

*Current Index to Journals in Education.* An indexing service to over 700 journals in education and related fields. Search by subject and author. Monthly.

*Current Law Index.* Indexes law journals and legal newspapers. Search by subjects, author/title, cases and statutes. Eight issues per year with quarterly and annual cumulations.

*Education Index.* Over 340 English-language journals relating to education. Search by subject and author. Monthly.

*Government Reports Announcements & Index.* Provides citations and abstracts of U.S. government agency reports made public through the National Technical Information Service. Search by subject. Semimonthly.

*Hospital Literature Index.* Index focuses on administrative issues. Search by subject or author. Quarterly.

*Human Resources Abstracts.* Abstracts on problems in cities. Search by topical headings. Quarterly.

*Index Medicus.* Index to world's literature in medicine. Search by subject. Monthly.

*Management Contents.* "Tables of Contents" to more than 320 business and management periodicals. Semimonthly.

*National Newspaper Index.* Covers *The New York Times, The Christian Science Monitor,* and *The Wall Street Journal.* Published on computer output microfilm. Search by Library of Congress subject headings. Updated monthly.

*New York Times Index.* A guide to the final day-edition of the *Times.* Search by subject. Semimonthly with quarterly and annual cumulations.

*PAIS Bulletin.* (Public Affairs Information Service Bulletin). Public affairs information of use to administrators and the business community. Covers 1,000 journals and state and federal government documents. Search by subject and author. Weekly.

*Personnel Literature.* Limited to materials received in the U.S. Office of Personnel Management. Includes books, journals, and government materials. Search by subject headings. Quarterly.

*Personnel Management Abstracts.* Books, journals, and government materials received by the Graduate School of Business Administration, University of Michigan. Search by subject headings. Quarterly.

*Sage Public Administration Abstracts.* Abstracts of over 120 journals on urban studies including government, transportation, education, finance, law, management, and the environment. Includes books, journal articles, pamphlets, government publications, legislative research studies and documents, state and local governments, program planning and evaluation, and personnel management. Search by categories. Quarterly.

*Social Sciences Index.* Covers over 350 periodicals in planning and public administration, police science and corrections, sociology, and urban studies. Search by author and subject. Quarterly.

*Statistical Reference Index.* Current statistical information from publications issued by business and commercial publishers. Search by subject and names. Bimonthly.

*Urban Affairs Abstracts.* Abstracts of urban literature. Search by subject. Weekly.

*Wall Street Journal Index.* Contains final eastern edition of *The Wall Street Journal.* Divided into Corporate News and General News. Search by subjects within each section. Monthly.

*Work-Related Abstracts.* A looseleaf service covering over 200 government and professional periodicals. Search by subjects. Monthly.

## SEARCH STRATEGY 11: PROFESSIONAL JOURNALS: HOW TO BROADEN YOUR READING

As a member of various organizations, it is likely that you routinely receive journals of interest to your business or profession. However, it is beneficial to broaden your reading in a content area.

Journals are expensive; browse through your library or collection center rather than subscribing to every journal of interest to you. In collections, journals are housed together in one location. They may be shelved by the Library of Congress Classification System or shelved alphabetically. A complete listing of journals and periodicals is in the annual *Ulrich's International Periodicals Directory.* (1932– ). New York: R. R. Bowker and in *The Standard Periodical Directory.* (1965/65– ). New York: Oxbridge Communications.

## SEARCH STRATEGY 12: GOVERNMENT PUBLICATIONS: AN OFTEN-OVERLOOKED SOURCE OF MATERIAL

Do not overlook the value of government documents. Most government documents are usually not listed in a library's online catalog system, so remember to consult the separate online computer system located within the government documents' section.

Government conducts hundreds of studies and generates reports at all levels: local, state, and federal. The Government Printing Office (GPO) publishes over 30,000 documents each year, available in libraries and through mail-order requests.

Depository libraries are found in academic or public libraries, and those libraries designated as depository libraries are listed in the September issue of the *Monthly Catalog*, the most current guide to the Government Printing Office's publications.

## SEARCH STRATEGY 13: LOCATING GOVERNMENT DOCUMENTS

Every collection must have an orderly arrangement of material. The publications issued by the many agencies of the U.S. government also are assigned a classification number or call number for easy retrieval. This is the Superintendent of Documents' Classification number, referred to as the "SuDoc" number.

Publications are grouped together by issuing agency. For example, all publications issued by the Labor Department are classified under "L," signifying Labor Department. Below is the classification system:

A—Agriculture Department
C—Commerce Department

C3—Census Bureau (Commerce Department)

D—Defense Department

E—Energy Department

GA—General Accounting Department

GS—General Services Administration

HE—Health and Human Services

I—Interior Department

J—Justice Department

L—Labor Department

NAS—National Aeronautics and Space Administration

S—State Department

T—Treasury Department

X-Y—Congress

Government documents are often confusing to locate; however, many libraries use CD-ROMs (Compact-disk read-only-memory) which have made retrieval easier. Silver-Platter and Autographics are two companies producing CD-ROMs geared toward retrieving government documents. These companies list all publications from the *Monthly Catalog,* and access is by author, title, subject, and keywords as well as SuDoc number or report number.

There are several good publications to consult when using government documents, especially on the organization of documents, that is, who issues what. However, with the use of the *Monthly Catalog* and CD-ROM searching, this is not as crucial as it was in the past. However, the following are several publications that aid in the understanding and searching of government documents:

Andriot, John. (1973– ). *Guide to U.S. Government Publications.* McLean, Va.: Documents Index. A guide to government series and periodicals currently being published.

Andriot, John. (1973). *Guide to U.S. Government Statistics.* 4th ed. McLean, Va.: Documents Index. This guide locates statistics by departments and agencies.

*Government Reference Books.* (1988). Littleton, Colo.: Libraries Unlimited. Is an "authoritative annotated guide to atlases, bibliographies, catalogs . . . indexes, and other reference monographs issued by agencies of the United States government during the most recent two-year period."

McIlvaine, Betsy. (1983). *A Consumers', Researchers', and Students' Guide to Government Publications.* New York: H. W. Wilson. An overview of governmental publications.

## SEARCH STRATEGY 14: HANDBOOKS: A QUICK GUIDE TO A SUBJECT

Handbooks give you an understanding and overview of the literature. A handbook can be a ready reference to a field of study and can be a quick and easy resource. Those listed below illustrate the wide variety of subject areas available:

Altman, Edward L., ed. (1981). *Financial Handbook.* 5th ed. New York: Wiley. A comprehensive handbook primarily on the management of a business.

*Bankers Desk Reference.* (1978– ). Boston: Warren, Gorham & Lamont. An annual subject guide covering banking regulations, consumer credit, deposits, collections, and international banking. Glossary included.

Buell, Victor P., ed. (1986). *Handbook of Modern Marketing.* New York: McGraw-Hill. Handbook of customers services, staffing of organizations, and legal concerns.

*The County Year Book.* (1975– ). Washington, D.C.: National Association of Counties with International City Management Association. An annual sourcebook on county governments.

*Dentist's Desk Reference: Materials, Instruments and Equipment.* (1983). Chicago: American Dental Association. A comprehensive source of dental materials and instruments and equipment for the dental office.

Fallon, William K., ed. (1983). *AMA Management Handbook.* 2d ed. New York: American Management Association. Covers all areas of management.

Kendrick, John W. (1984). *Improving Company Productivity: Handbook with Case Studies.* Baltimore: Johns Hopkins University Press. Focuses on improving productivity by utilizing the case-study method.

*Municipal Year Book.* (1922– ). Washington, D.C.: International City Management Association. Annual developments in U.S. cities; statistics and trends.

Perry, J. L., ed. (1989). *Handbook of Public Administration.* San Francisco: Jossey-Bass. A comprehensive volume including budget preparation, performance evaluation, and interpersonal relationships.

Rabin, Jack, W. Bartley Hildreth, and Gerald J. Miller, eds. (1989). *Handbook of Public Administration.* New York: Dekker. Includes all areas of public administration from finance to personnel management.

Seidler, Lee J., and D. R. Carmichael, eds. (1981). *Accountants' Handbook.* New York: Wiley. A two-volume reference work to the field of accounting.

Tracey, William R., ed. (1985). *Human Resources Management and Development Handbook.* New York: American Management Association. A handbook for managing and developing human resources in your business or agency.

U.S. Bureau of the Census. (1879– ). *Statistical Abstract of the United States.* Washington, D.C.: Government Printing Office. An annual source of statistical information.

Washnis, George J., ed. (1979). *Productivity Improvement Handbook for State and Local Government.* New York: Wiley.

Techniques to improve productivity. This classic publication is currently under revision.

## SEARCH STRATEGY 15: COOPERATIVE SHARING: WHERE TO FIND MATERIALS NOT FOUND IN YOUR COLLECTION

Interlibrary loan services are available within all university libraries. Extensive networking among libraries has made more materials available through a sharing of resources. The procedure for requesting information is simple; usually within one week the material arrives from the holding library and is available for checkout. In times of scarce resources and increased publishing costs, sharing of resources has become an important and valued service of libraries.

## SEARCH STRATEGY 16: ONLINE DATABASE SEARCHING

Another service available is online computer searches. Online searching requires computer linkage via telecommunications to a machine-readable database. Online searching involves the use of a database, a complete collection of records capable of being read by a computer. A database evolves from a "field," and a field is a part of a record; that is, an author, a title, or a call number. A record is a unit of information containing several fields considered as one. For example, a bibliographic citation may be considered one record made up of several fields, for instance, author, publisher, call number, subject heading, or others. The database comprises a complete collection of these records, readable by a computer.

Many academic and research libraries offer online computer searchers for a fee. A trained searcher within the facility will search sources for you. Although having a searcher prepare a bibliography saves time, this search should not be a substitute for your library search; it should be conducted in conjunction with it. The computerized searches are expensive, often costing $100 or more per hour on one database.

## SEARCH STRATEGY 17: FORMULATING YOUR ONLINE SEARCH STATEMENT

Great care and time should be spent in formulating the search request or search statement. The expertise of the searcher is utilized through the information given. Your search statement should be concise and should reflect specifically the information you are seeking.

A search request should contain the following information:

*Title of search.* The searcher writes out search request.

*Statement of the question.* The searcher is asked to detail or elaborate on the information requested. Often this involves a restatement of the problem.

*Important terms, synonyms, keywords, phrases, concepts, authors.* The online computer will search using these keywords and authors known to have written on the topic.

*Years covered.* The search may be limited in time, perhaps to information written within the previous five years only.

*Databases to be searched.* The searchers may request specific databases to be searched.

*Language limitations.* The searcher may want only English-language citations.

## SEARCH STRATEGY 18: KNOWING WHAT DATABASES ARE AVAILABLE

The major companies in online searching are BRS (Bibliographic Retrieval Services), DIALOG (DIALOG Information

Services, Inc.) and ORBIT (SDC Search Service). Although there are thousands of databases available, a few are:

*ABI Inform.* Management and administration in the United States and abroad.

*American Statistical Index.* Statistical information collected by the U.S. Government.

*Comprehensive Dissertation Index.* Citations of doctoral dissertations and masters theses.

*Congressional Information Service.* Abstracts of publications issued by House and Senate and Joint Committees of Congress.

*Congressional Record Abstracts.* Coverage of the *Congressional Record.*

*Criminal Justice Periodical Index.* Indexes journals on criminal justice and law enforcement.

*Dissertation Abstracts.* Citations to dissertations.

*Dow Jones News/Retrieval.* News and current information. Full text of *The Wall Street Journal, Barron's, Business Week, Forbes, Fortune, Money.* The QuickSearch command obtains all information with a low fee each time it is utilized.

*ERIC.* Journal articles dealing with education.

*Federal Index.* Proposed rules, regulations, bills, speeches in the *Congressional Record, Federal Register, U.S. Code,* and *The Washington Post.*

*Federal Register.* Coverage of the *Federal Register.* Includes rules, proposed rules, meetings, hearings, executive orders, and presidential proclamations.

*GPO Monthly Catalog.* All unclassified documents produced by the Government Printing Office or at government expense.

*Harvard Business Review Online.* Journal articles in the *Harvard Business Review.*

*Legal Resource Index.* Indexes legal journals and newspapers.

*LEXIS/NEXIS.* Legal and business news. Over 400 regional, national, and international news and business sources included as well as federal and state cases, federal and state statutes, tax cases, insurance law, and law reviews.

*Local Government Information Network* (LOGIN). Covers urban practices and ways to improve these practices and problems in local government.

*Management Contents.* Covers accounting, business, economics, management, and public administration.

*National Criminal Justice Retrieval Service.* Covers literature of criminal justice and law enforcement.

*National Newspaper Index.* Indexes *The New York Times, The Wall Street Journal,* and *The Christian Science Monitor.*

*National Technical Info Service* (NTIS). Unclassified technical reports of U.S. government–sponsored research.

*Newsnet.* Current business information. Includes access to over 350 business newsletters as well as company profiles.

*Newsearch.* The Daily Index: Indexes periodicals, newspapers in *Legal Resource Index,* and journals in *Management Contents.*

*Online Microcomputer Software Guide and Directory.* Software and its producers.

*Psychological Abstracts.* Summaries of the world's literature in psychology and related fields.

*Public Affairs Information Service* (PAIS). Publications in social science, public affairs, and economics.

*Social Science Citation Index.* Contents of journals in the social sciences.

*Sociological Abstracts.* Covers the literature of sociology.

*TRAINET.* Provides access to training information. Includes conferences, seminars, and workshops as well as course material.

*WESTLAW.* Full text of federal case law, statutes and regulations, and selected law reviews.

*Online Bibliographic Databases: A Directory and Sourcebook* (Hall 1986). Lists the following additional databases:

| | |
|---|---|
| *ACCOUNTANTS' INDEX* | accountancy |
| *ACOMPLINE* | urban matters |
| *AGRICOLA* | agriculture |
| *AGRIS* | agriculture |
| *AP NEWS* | news |
| *BANKER* | banking |
| *BMA PRESS CUTTINGS* | medicine |
| *CA SEARCH* | chemistry |
| *CAS ONLINE* | chemistry |
| *CATLINE* | medicine |
| *CHEMICAL BUSINESS NEWSBASE* | chemistry |
| *CHEMICAL HAZARDS IN INDUSTRY* | chemical hazards |
| *CISDOC* | occupational health |
| *CIS/INDEX* | U.S. Congress |
| *CLAIMS/US PATENT FILES* | patents |
| *COMPENDEX* | engineering |
| *COMPUTER DATABASE* | computers |
| *DHSS DATA* | health and social security |
| *DOE ENERGY* | energy |
| *ECONOMIC LITERATURE INDEX* | economics |
| *ELECTRONIC PUBLISHING ABSTRACTS* | publishing |
| *EMBASE* | medicine |
| *ENERGYLINE* | energy |
| *ENVIROLINE* | environment |
| *FINANCIAL INDUSTRY INFO SER* | finance |
| *INDUSTRY DATA SOURCES* | industry |
| *INFOBANK* | news |
| *INPADOC* | patents |

| | |
|---|---|
| *INSURANCE ABSTRACTS* | insurance |
| *LABORDOC* | labor |
| *MICROCOMPUTER INDEX* | microcomputers |
| *NEWSEARCH* | news |
| *NEXIS* | interdisciplinary |
| *OCCUPATIONAL SAFETY AND HEALTH* | safety |
| *PREDICASTS INDEXES* | business |
| *TRADE AND INDUSTRY INDEX* | business |
| *UPI NEWS* | news |

Online database searching is used by many governmental agencies, law firms, corporations, accounting firms, and medical facilities. Since there are over 5,000 databases available, the following publications will assist in deciding those databases useful to your business or agency:

*Data Base Directory.* (1984/85– ). White Plains, N.Y.: Knowledge Industry Publications. An annual publication listing pricing, vendor, and content information.

*Datapro Directory of On-Line Services.* (1985). Delran, N.J.: Datapro Research Corp. A two-volume, loose-leaf service of database information.

*Directory of Online Databases.* (1979– ). Santa Monica, Calif.: Cuadra Associates. An alphabetical listing of database services including vendor and ordering information.

Williams, Martha E., ed. (1985). *Computer-Readable Databases: A Directory and Data Sourcebook.* Chicago: American Library Association. A comprehensive two-volume guide to over 5,000 databases. Includes subject and producer indexes.

There are many useful guides available for mastering the techniques of online searching. Many of these guides are quite technical; however, the two listed below are good for the beginner searcher.

Byerly, Greg. (1983). *Online Searching: A Dictionary and Bibliographic Guide.* Littleton, Colo.: Libraries Unlimited. A guide to online searching with definitions and a selective annotated bibliography.

Howitt, Doran, and Marvin I. Weinberger. (1984). *Inc. Magazine's Databasics: Your Guide to Online Business Information.* New York: Garland Publishing. A valuable guide for business information.

## SEARCH STRATEGY 19: CD-ROM SEARCHING

CD-ROM makes available searching with the compact-disk format. The database is stored on a compact disk, and searching the database utilizes the same keyword techniques as online searching. This is another efficient and time-saving means of acquiring information other than references in print. The disk is purchased and used as an in-house source.

Several of the CD-ROM databases are:

*ABI/Inform.* Covers business and management topics.

*Applied Science & Technology Index.* Covers all areas of technology from 1983 to present.

*Biological & Agricultural Index.* Covers all areas of biology and agriculture from 1983 to present.

*ERIC.* Index with abstracts to journals in education from 1966 to present.

*NTIS* database. Index to the most recent five years of information from the National Technical Information Service covering government-sponsored research and development reports.

*OSH-ROM* database. From the National Institute for Occupational Safety and Health.

*PAIS.* Covers information on public affairs from around the world from books, reports, government publications, and journals.

*PHINet Tax Resources.* Covers tax-law regulations, cases, and rulings.

*PsycLit.* Index with abstracts to articles from psychology journals, 1981 to present.

Information Access Company, the H. W. Wilson Company, Dialog Information Services, and SilverPlatter Information are main suppliers of CD-ROMs. These companies and some of their databases are listed below.

INFOTRAC, by Information Access Company, offers a compact system of CD-ROM databases:

*The Academic Index* (social science, science)

*General Periodicals Index* (social science, business)

*Government Publications Index* (government)

*LegalTrac* (law)

*National Newspaper Index* (news)

The H. W. Wilson Company produces *WilsonDisc*, including:

*Applied Science and Technology Index* (science/technology)

*Business Periodicals Index* (business)

*Education Index* (education)

*General Science Index* (science)

*Index to Legal Periodicals* (law)

*Social Science Index* (social science)

Dialog Information Services has the DiaLOG ONDisc line of CD-ROM products:

*ERIC* (education)

*MEDLINE* (medicine)

*NTIS* (government)

SilverPlatter Information, Inc., produces the following on CD-ROM databases:

*ERIC* (education)
*PsycLit* (psychology/behavioral science)
*AV Online* (audiovisual)
*Sociofile* (sociology)
*MEDLINE* (medicine)
*NTIS* (government)
*OSH-ROM* (occupational safety/health)
*AGRICOLA* (agriculture)

Additional information on available databases in the CD-ROM format may be found in the following publications:

Emard, Jean-Paul. (1988). *CD-ROMs in Print 1988–1989: An International Guide.* Westport, Conn.: Meckler Corporation. A guide to all available CD-ROMs.

Nelson, Nancy. (1987). *CD-ROMs in Print.* Westport, Conn.: Meckler Corporation. A useful glossary as well as product name information.

## SEARCH STRATEGY 20: UTILIZING YOUR PERSONAL COMPUTER IN SEARCHING

Just as firms or companies connect via computers and telephones to large databases, so can the individual, at home or at the office. The three major online computer companies (Dialog, BRS, and SCD/Orbit) produce online databases for use after peak hours.

In addition to those online databases previously listed, the following databases are less expensive than the larger databases and therefore are oriented towards the individual consumer.

## BRS/AFTER DARK

Includes thirty databases of interest to doctors, attorneys, and the business world. The searching fee is less than $25 per hour. It is very easy to use with both a menu or direct command searching capabilities. It includes the following databases:

*ABI/INFORM* (business)

*ACADEMIC AMERICAN ENCYCLOPEDIA DATABASE* (multidisciplinary)

*AGRICOLA* (agriculture)

*BOOKS IN PRINT* (U.S. books)

*ENERGY DATABASE* (energy/environment)

*ERIC* (education)

*HARVARD BUSINESS REVIEW/ONLINE* (business)

*HEALTH PLANNING AND ADMINISTRATION DATABASE* (health)

*MANAGEMENT CONTENTS* (business)

*MEDLARS-ON-LINE AND BACKFILES* (medicine, dentistry, nursing)

*PUBLIC AFFAIRS INFORMATION SERVICE* (social science)

## CompuServe

This system contains hundreds of databases and is easy to use with little or no training required. It allows the searcher to use menus or to search directly. Primarily for professionals and people in the business world, it is relatively inexpensive, costing less than $10 per hour. It includes the following databases:

*AP PRESS NEWS* (news)

*BUSINESS INFORMATION WIRE* (business)

*INVESTMENT NEWS AND VIEWS* (investments)
*NEWSPAPERS* (news)
*QUICK QUOTE* (finance)
*VALUE LINE DATA BASE II* (business)

## DELPHI

Delphi is a communications and information package for business and personal information. It can send and receive mail. It gives business and financial information as well as offering a research service. At less than $10 per hour, it is in the inexpensive category.

## KNOWLEDGE INDEX

This system is primarily for professionals and people in the business world. It is easy to use and inexpensive, costing less than $25 per hour. Its databases are:

*ABI/INFORM* (business)
*AGRICOLA* (agriculture)
*BOOKS IN PRINT* (U.S. books)
*ERIC* (education)
*LEGAL RESOURCE INDEX* (law)
*MAGAZINE INDEX* (multidisciplinary)
*NATIONAL NEWSPAPER INDEX* (news)
*NEWSEARCH* (news)
*TRADE AND INDUSTRY INDEX* (index to trade and industry journals)

## THE SOURCE

Hundreds of databases on news, finance, business and education. Inexpensive, especially after prime-time hours, it costs less than $20 per hour.

## SELF-DIRECTED IMPROVEMENT STRATEGIES

On a recent visit to a local law firm, I saw firsthand an information center at work. It was a hub of activity. Books and law journals were being consulted. Computers were connected via telecommunications to search huge databases. In-house CD-ROMs were rapidly seeking out additional information. This is the reality of information retrieval in companies today.

Information is readily available at one's fingertips. Whether you thumb through an indexing or abstracting service or access information via a computer, the search strategies presented in this chapter will help you develop skills for retrieving valuable information. Successful managers or professionals can master these strategies with ease and readily put them to work. Here are a few suggestions for getting started.

### Use This Guide

The first suggestion for developing information search skill is simply to use this chapter as a guide and undertake a hands-on search. Select one or two specific strategies and a topic of interest and then head to a library or a computer modem.

### Guided Tour

Major libraries often have regularly scheduled tours or will provide a personalized tour. Arrange to tour a library facility, armed with questions about how to manage a search process.

### Reference Librarian

A good reference librarian can be a valuable instructor. Take advantage of this resource not just to assist in one search, but as a way to learn how information is organized and how it can be accessed.

## Search Specialist as Consultant Turned Teacher

Early online computer searches are best done with the assistance of a search specialist. Participate in the search along with the specialist and use it as a learning opportunity as well as a way to conduct a specific search. Questions about search technique should be well received. If not, find another specialist to work with.

## Books

Alberico, Ralph. (1987). *Microcomputers for the Online Searcher.* Westport, Conn.: Meckler. Requires a knowledge of basic principles of automated retrieval.

Bowen, C., and D. Peyton. (1984). *How to Get the Most out of CompuServe.* New York: Bantam. Detailed explanation of CompuServe, including searching techniques.

Cane, Mike. (1985). *The Computer Phone Book.* New York: New American Library. Explores several hundred Bulletin Board Systems as well as CompuServe and BRS/AFTER DARK systems for personal computer use.

Glossbrenner, Alfred. (1983). *The Complete Handbook of Personal Computer Communications: Everything You Need to Go Online with the World.* New York: St. Martin's Press. Comprehensive guide to making your personal computer work for you. Includes The Source, CompuServe, and Delphi systems for your personal computer.

Hansen, Carol. (1984). *A Microcomputer User's Guide to Information Online.* Hasbrouck Heights, N.J.: Hayden Book Company. Good general guide to microcomputer access of online communications.

Kieffer, Tom. (1984). *Get Connected: A Guide to Telecommunications.* Culver City, Calif.: Ashton-Tate. A good starter book for online searching requirements.

Lewis, Sasha. (1984). *Plugging In: The Microcomputerist's Guide to Telecommunications.* Radnor, Pa.: Chilton. Another good book for the beginner to use when thinking about how to use the computer for communicating.

Nilles, Jack. (1983). *Micro and Modems: Telecommunicating With Personal Computers.* Reston, Va.: Reston Publishing. More-technical approach to using your personal computer to its fullest potential.

Shafritz, Jay M., and Louise Alexander. (1984). *The Reston Directory of On-Line Databases, Your Computer's Phone Book: A Travel Guide to the World of Information that Can Be Called Up on Any Computer.* Reston, Va.: Reston Publishing. Complete guide to online databases for access by your computer.

Stone, M. David. (1984). *Getting On-Line: A Guide to Accessing Computer Information Services.* Englewood Cliffs, N.J.: Prentice-Hall. Detailed description is included for eleven systems including BRS/AFTER DARK, CompuServe, Delphi, and KNOWLEDGE INDEX.

## Catalogs from Vendors

Send for catalogs from vendors and use them as an introduction to the resources available and the search techniques used and hardware required.

## Subscribe to Online Information Service

Take the plunge and subscribe to an information service. Then use it.

# REFERENCES

Granick, Lois, Alain Y. Dessaint, and Gary R. VandenBos. (1990). "How Information Systems Can Help Build Professional Competence." In Sherry L. Willis and Samuel S. Dubin, eds., *Maintaining Professional Competence: Approaches to Career Enhancement, Vitality, and Success Throughout a Work Life*. San Francisco: Jossey-Bass, 278–305.

Hall, James. (1986). *Online Bibliographic Databases: A Directory and Sourcebook*. 4th ed. London: Aslib.

# 8

## Learning: Making Skill Development a Lifelong Habit

A skill with any depth can never be fully mastered; there is always room for more improvement. That is clearly the case with the six skill areas in this book. The inability to master them completely, however, is a positive, not a negative feature. When growth stops, decline sets in. The inability to totally master a skill area means there is continuing opportunity for growth. Without it, we would regress.

The potential for continuing growth in each skill is a reason it can maintain our interest. The ideal is to move to a level of competence and then continue to improve on it for a lifetime. Given the important role these generic skills play in our ability to function effectively in our professional and personal lives, making them a lifetime pursuit is a worthy undertaking.

### TOTAL LIFE-STYLE PERSPECTIVE

Rather than simply thinking of learning, including skills development, as something that occurs as part of our professional lives, think of them as part of total life-style. What contribution can skill development make to our personal and leisure goals as well as professional ones? This perspective is one aspect of planning for total life-style. Midcareer professionals and public managers will gain perspective about career decisions if they think and plan not just for a career but for a life-style that includes career as one major component. While that may, on the surface, appear obvious, it is not always done. Especially in a group of ambitious people who have career aspirations in common, there is a tendency to get excited about career goals, including ones that would require giving up personal goals that might have equal validity. Career is important, but not everything. Starting with an effort to visualize future desired life-style can be a healthy antidote to one-sided ambition that might later become derailed simply because it is too costly in the sacrifices required. The positive feature of the life-style perspective regarding continuing learning is that learning can contribute to and be part of the noncareer portions of our lives.

These six skills have enough depth that, for the person who wishes to pursue them, they can take on an avocational meaning of their own. It is possible to "turn on" to one or more of these skills. Rather than simply writing better memos at work, begin or increase the amount of writing you do for professional publication. Move the writing venture out of the professional arena and begin to write in other topic areas: how-to or entertaining publications related to a hobby, or short stories, or a novel. Writing better memos and reports is a worthy goal in itself, but it is not the only achievable writing goal.

Public speaking, and the other skill areas, may carry well beyond the workplace. It is quite possible to move from effective speaking in a professional organization to speaking to outside groups right on to the professional speaking tour. These rather grand uses of the generic skills are not likely for most of us, but it is nice to realize that such options are available.

## SKILL DEVELOPMENT AS A CONTINUING ACTIVITY

How can you place skill development on your agenda and make it a continuing activity and commitment? How can you build some enthusiasm for learning to become a better writer, or speaker, or one who relates more effectively to others, without the enthusiasm going the way of most New Year's resolutions and diets?

It is easy to discover a new project and rush off in its pursuit with great enthusiasm. Millions of unfulfilled New Year's resolutions are testimony to this phenomenon. And diets started. And exercise programs abandoned. The trick is to maintain the effort, along with some of the enthusiasm, after the project is underway, when it is work and no longer new. There are no guarantees, but here are a few ideas.

### Hobby

Some people quite successfully adopt one of these skills as a hobby in its own right. Some computer buffs, for example, make computing and tinkering with a computer a major form of leisure activity. If this level of interest is generated, it is likely to be sustained for a period of time.

### Contributor to Hobby

Although not considered hobbies in themselves, these skills might be a regular important contributor or adjunct to a hobby you do pursue regularly. I know a couple who are active members of an international network of hiking/walking clubs. Part of the attraction of their nearly weekly walks in different parts of the country or world is meeting new people and learning something about them. Interviewing skill is an important contributor to their hobby.

### Collaborative Learning

Learning often can be more effective in a group, and sustaining an activity usually benefits from the support of others. Joining a formal group is a possibility for many, if not all of these skills. It is also possible to build your own group. Find some persons, or perhaps only one, who share the interest. A biweekly lunch meeting or some other contact can provide an opportunity to compare notes and a stimulus to continue. Even leisure activities work best with a support group to share the pleasure and the frustration.

### Try a New Activity or Approach

Variety is an important contributor to the maintenance of interest and enthusiasm. Whatever the learning activity, try something new on occasion. If your strategy to learn computing is to pursue a certificate in microcomputer applications at a university requiring eight courses, take a semester off in the middle and devote the time to learning some new features on your own that the formal program does not include.

### Rotate the Skill Receiving Emphasis

It is usually not possible to give an adequate amount of attention to all of these skill areas and the other matters that need attending. At any given time, one or two will probably receive the most attention. Rotating that one or two provides some variety.

### Set Measurable Goals and Measure Progress

Having a way to track progress can add significantly to your ability to sustain interest in skill development. In principle, it is possible to measure progress in all of these skill areas. Even so, it is not as simple as keeping track of your time in the 10K run. Still, it can be done. Writing can be measured in amount, or with a scale of quality like that suggested for self-feedback. Some interviewers maintain a simple rating sheet to score their own performances after each interview. A specific list of programs to learn can provide goals and a measure of progress in the computing area.

### Importance of Application

As you develop in a skill, apply it in a useful way. Not only does the application offer practice opportunity, it also builds in psychological reinforcement that the skill has useful payoffs.

### Leisure Skill as Model

Let me give you a reason to take up skiing and move from novice to expert. Actually, any sport or hobby will do as long as it is a skill and you are not already good at it. Use that leisure skill as an exercise to study your own pattern of skill development. Several things might happen. First, you might become enamored with the enjoyment of developing a new skill. Beginning fresh at something and then moving through the kind of stages laid out in chapter 1 can be a fascinating project. Second, it can provide insights into other skill development. One difficulty with writing, speaking, and so forth is that most of us already have a lot of "baggage" associated with them. We are not starting any of them anew, so the pure experience of moving from nothing to mastery is not possible. I cannot guarantee that your ski lessons will be tax deductible as a required part of your professional training but I will bet on your gaining some interesting insight.

### Stretching Experience

Developing a high level of mastery of any one or several of these skills can be what I call a "stretching" experience, one that takes you far enough out of your normal routine to be mildly uncomfortable. One beauty of a stretching experience is that it makes us more likely to seek out others. Learning to speak effectively can help create an attitude that leads to some other professional effort that had previously been uncomfortable enough that we did not want to do it. And for the third benefit of the ski lessons: if you reach the point that you can ski full-bore down the expert slope, you will probably be willing to speak to an audience of any size. One stretching experience does lead to another. Those stretching experiences are an important ingredient of professional vitality.

### Positive Reinforcement

Throughout the skill development effort, look for positive reinforcement. Some of that may be internal, feeling good about your accomplishments, for instance. Some of it may be external, such as praise from co-workers or rewards on the job. Some may fall in between, you providing rewards for yourself. After you master the ability to find even the most fugitive of documents, to complete a computer analysis of alternative budget proposals, to bring a new level of energy and openness to your work group, to complete a successful job interview resulting in a major career move, to give a superb presentation to the executive committee, or to finish the final revisions for a book, treat yourself to a trip to the Alps.